PETRARCH'S VISIONS
AND THEIR
RENAISSANCE ANALOGUES

José Porrúa Turanzas, S.A.
EDICIONES

stuðía humanítatís

Petrarch's Visions and their Renaissance Analogues

BY

JULIA CONAWAY BONDANELLA

studia humanitatis

PUBLISHER, PRINTER AND DISTRIBUTOR
José Porrúa Turanzas, S. A.
Cea Bermúdez, 10 - Madrid-3
España

© JULIA CONAWAY BONDANELLA

Dep. legal M. 16.577.-1978

I. S. B. N. 84-7317-072-5

IMPRESO EN ESPAÑA
PRINTED IN SPAIN

Ediciones José Porrúa Turanzas, S. A.
Cea Bermúdez, 10 - Madrid-3

_____

TALLERES GRÁFICOS PORRÚA, S. A.
JOSÉ, 10 - MADRID-29

To my family

TABLE OF CONTENTS

Page

JAN VAN DER NOOT'S, *A Theatre for Worldlings* (London, 1569). This
woodcut illustrates the second poem of the «Epigrams» by Edmund
Spenser, which corresponds to lines 13-23 of Petrarch's Canzone 323.

PREFACE

The purpose of the present study is to investigate a family of poems derived from Petrarch's *canzone*, «Standomi un giorno solo a la fenestra,» a poem composed some twenty years after the death of his beloved Laura. It figures in the second part of the *Canzoniere*. This curious *canzone* presents a series of six symbolic visions in which the poet watches six of the most beautiful earthly creatures or creations come to an unexpected end. Because of its finely wrought images, «Standomi un giorno» furnished inspiration for artists in other media, including the author of the first emblem book in England. It can be placed in a long tradition of vision poetry and it recalls the particularly medieval tradition of meditations on death. Whatever the traditions it echoes, this poem, from a stylistic and thematic point of view, is related both to Petrarch's Latin works and to his Italian verses, love lyrics and *Triumphs*.

Within the framework of the *Canzoniere*, «Standomi un giorno» is somewhat atypical; it does not offer the poetic representation of the inner life of the poet, but rather evokes his emotional shock over his lady's death in a more emblematic manner. At the same time, its visionary nature, its symbolic tableaux, and the resulting distancing make it less and less at home in the developing Renaissance; it is somewhat on the margin

— 1 —

of the main current of sixteenth-century Petrarchism. Yet, it is true that four important Renaissance poets, Marot, Du Bellay, van der Noot, and Spenser took a special interest in «Standomi un giorno,» and they found it adaptable to their own languages, their native poetic traditions, and their personal poetic visions. This remains a surprising phenomenon for a twentieth-century reader, and it has seemed worthwhile to explore how and why this particular *canzone* appealed to these four major European poets and the manner in which each utilized it for his own ends.

My aim has been to suggest a framework within which this vision poetry may best be read and an approach to lyrics which have been judged largely outside the context of their individual «family.» My analyses begin with a brief general examination of the cultural and literary factors which worked on the poet of *canzone* 323, rather than with a theory about why «Standomi un giorno» was imitated. By way of specific examples, I have tried to suggest what these poems hold in common, their «family resemblances,» to use Wittgenstein's term, and where the individual contributions lie. This essay tries to illuminate different facets of a single central problem, why this particular *canzone* was imitated, while relying on a single approach, that of comparison and contrast. The common faith of these poets in artistic conventions is central to this examination of «Standomi un giorno» and its analogues. In the individual chapters, the emphasis and choice are personal. After studying the poems, the criticism, and the considerable volume of historical information, I have concentrated only on those aspects of literary history, taste, and individual style which seemed most pertinent to this study of one aspect of Petrarchism.

Anyone who writes about Petrarch is conscious of his debt to those who have written about Petrarch before. The debt is large and while some debts are acknowledged explicitly in the notes, others are not, since I could not logically refer to them. It would serve little purpose in a work of such specific limits to express in detail my obligations to the numerous general works on Petrarchism.

It remains to write a word of thanks to Dr. Chandler Beall, who suggested this topic and has patiently advised me in the course of my work. And I am glad to express my gratitude also to Dr. Walter N. King from whom I learned an appreciation of Renaissance literature as well as to Dr. Thomas R. Hart, whose guidance in research and writing has been continually helpful. Finally, I must acknowledge the aid and encouragement of my husband Peter, without which I could never have completed this task.

CHAPTER I

A BRIEF BACKGROUND TO PETRARCH'S CANZONE CCCXXIII

Standomi un giorno solo a la fenestra,
  Onde cose vedea tante e sí nove
  Ch'era sol di mirar quasi già stanco,
  Una fera m'apparve da man destra
  Con fronte umana da far arder Giove,
  Cacciata da duo veltri, un nero, un bianco;
  Che l'un e l'altro fianco
  De la fera gentil mordean sí forte,
  Che 'n poco tempo la menaro al passo,
  Ove chiusa in un sasso
  Vinse molta bellezza acerba morte:
  E mi fe' sospirar sua dura sorte.

Indi per alto mar vidi una nave
  Con le sarte di seta e d'òr la vela,
  Tutta d'avorio e d'ebeno contesta:
  E 'l mar tranquillo e l'aura era soave,
  E 'l ciel qual è se nulla nube il vela:
  Ella carca di ricca merce onesta:
  Poi repente tempesta
  Orïental turbò sí l'aere e l'onde
  Che la nave percosse ad uno scoglio.
  O che grave cordoglio!

Breve ora oppresse e poco spazio asconde
L'alte ricchezze a null'altre seconde.

In un boschetto novo i rami santi
    Fiorian d'un lauro giovenetto e schietto,
    Ch'un de li arbor parea di paradiso;
    E di sua ombra uscian sí dolci canti
    Di vari augelli e tant'altro diletto,
    Che dal mondo m'avean tutto diviso:
    E mirando 'l io fiso
    Cangiossi 'l cielo in torno, e tinto in vista
    Folgorando 'l percosse, e da radice
    Quella pianta felice
    Subito svelse: onde mia vita è trista,
    Ché simile ombra mai non si racquista.

Chiara fontana in quel medesmo bosco
    Sorgea d'un sasso, et acque fresche e dolci
    Spargea, soavemente mormorando:
    Al bel seggio riposto, ombroso e fosco,
    Né pastori appressavan né bifolci,
    Ma ninfe e muse, a quel tenor cantando:
    Ivi m'assisi; e quando
    Piú dolcezza prendea di tal concento
    E di tal vista, aprir vidi uno speco
    E portarsene seco
    La fonte e 'l loco: ond'ancor doglia sento,
    E sol de la memoria mi sgomento.

Una strania fenice, ambedue l'ale
    Di porpora vestita e 'l capo d'oro,
    Vedendo per la selva, altera e sola,
    Veder forma celeste et immortale
    Prima pensai, fin ch'a lo svelto alloro
    Giunse et al fonte che la terra invola:
    Ogni cosa al fin vola:
    Ché, mirando le frondi a terra sparse

E 'l troncon rotto e quel vivo umor secco,
Volse in sé stessa il becco
Quasi sdegnando, e 'n un punto disparse:
Onde 'l cor di pietate e d'amor m'arse.

Al fin vid'io per entro i fiori e l'erba
Pensosa ir sí leggiadra e bella donna,
Che mai no 'l penso ch'i' non arda e treme,
Umile in sé, ma 'n contra Amor superba;
Et avea in dosso sí candida gonna,
Sí testa, ch'oro e neve parea inseme;
Ma le parti supreme
Eran avolte d'una nebbia oscura:
Punta poi nel tallon d'un picciol angue,
Come fior còlto langue,
Lieta si dipartío, non che secura:
Ahi nulla altro che pianto al mondo dura!

Canzon, tu puoi ben dire:
—Queste sei visïoni al signor mio
Han fatto un dolce di morir desio.— (1)

Many studies have been written on the influence of
Petrarch's love lyrics in Europe. Most of these are historical
or primarily concerned with the more introspective and
psychologically profound poems. (2) A few have concentrated

---

(1) All quotations from the *Canzoniere* are taken from Giosuè
Carducci and Severino Ferrari, eds., *Le Rime di Francesco Petrarca*
(Florence: Sansoni, 1899), and will henceforth be indicated in the
text proper by poem number and lines. All italics are my own. A
portion of the first two chapters of the present study has already
appeared as an article entitled «Petrarch as Visionary: The Import
of Canzone 323» in Aldo Scaglione, ed. *Francis Petrarch, Six
Centuries Later: A Symposium*, Univ. of North Carolina Studies in
the Romance Langs. and Lits.: Symposia No. 3 (Chapel Hill: Univ.
of North Carolina Press, 1975), pp. 117-127.
(2) Such works as J. Vianey's *Le Pétrarquisme en France au
siezième siècle* (Montpellier: Coulet, 1909), Henri Hauvette's *Les*

upon the stylistic aspects of Petrarchism or upon families of sonnets derived from particular poems. (3) One such group of poems, based on the *canzone* «Standomi un giorno solo a la fenestra,» has never received a comprehensive treatment. It fell into neglect when its medieval, allegorical flavor, its visionary structure, and its procession of figures of mutability ceased to be in fashion. Yet, it is precisely these features which made it attractive to its age and to its imitators of the Renaissance. In view of the current revival of interest in the lyrics of Petrarch, a study of this *canzone* seems appropriate and overdue.

In its best sense, the term «Petrarchism» refers to the style of Petrarch's lyric poetry and that of his imitators in Italy and abroad from the fourteenth to the early seventeenth centuries. It has too often been reserved for the abuses, the

---

Poésies lyriques de Pétrarque (Paris: Malfère, 1931), J. Scott-Espiner's *Les Sonnets elisabéthains: Les Sources et l'Apport personnel* (Paris: Champion, 1929), George Watson's *The English Petrarchans: A Critical Bibliography of the Canzoniere*, Warburg Institute Surveys, III (London: Univ. of London Press, 1967), and Anthony Mortimer's *Petrarch's Canzoniere in the English Renaissance* (Rome: Minerva Italica, 1975) furnish valuable information on the sources the Petrarchan poets used. Other studies, such as L. C. John's *The Elizabethan Sonnet Sequences: Studies in Conventional Conceits* (New York: Columbia Univ. Press, 1938), J. W. Lever's *The Elizabethan Love Sonnet* (London: Methuen, 1956), David Kalstone's *Sidney's Poetry: Contexts and Interpretations* (Cambridge: Harvard Univ. Press, 1965), Donald Stone's *Ronsard's Sonnet Cycles: A Study in Tone and Vision* (New Haven: Yale Univ. Press, 1966), Donald Guss's *John Donne, Petrarchist: Italianate Conceits and Love Theory in the «Songs and Sonets»* (Detroit: Wayne State Univ. Press, 1966), Luzius Keller's *Übersetzung und Nachahmung im europäischen Petrarkismus: Studien und Texte* (Stuttgart: J. B. Metzler, 1974), and several essays in Aldo Scaglione, ed., *Francis Petrarch*, treat the influence of Petrarchism on particular European poets.

(3) Examples of such studies are Joseph Fucilla, «Superbi colli: Notas sobre la boga del tema en España» in *Superbi colli e altri saggi* (Rome: Carucci Editore, 1963), pp. 7-43; R. O. Jones, «Renaissance Butterfly, Mannerist Flea: Tradition and Change in Renaissance Poetry,» *MLN*, 80 (1965), 166-184; and Joseph Fucilla, «Materials for the History of a Popular Classical Theme» in his *Studies and Notes (Literary and Historical)* (Naples: Istituto Editoriale del Mezzogiorno, n. d.).

artificialities of this style. In the studies of such critics as Franco Simone, the term «Petrarchism» is currently acquiring its broadest significance and is coming to mean, in the field of poetry, the dominant literary style of the European Renaissance. (4)

Although often called the first «modern man,» (5) Petrarch shared and voiced the concerns of his contemporaries. The terrible plague of 1348, in which Laura died, influences Petrarch's whole outlook on life; it is the inspiration for the tenth Latin eclogue, and one of the major occasions commemorated in the poetry of the *Trionfi* and the *Canzoniere*. His immediate response to the Black Death, seen in a Latin letter written at this time, shows a medieval awareness of man's mortality, as well as a modern human preoccupation with his own individual fate:

Alas, what lies before me? Whither now
Am I to be whirled away by the force of fate?
Time rushes onward for the perishing world,
And round about I see the hosts of the dying,
The young and the old; nor is there anywhere
In all the world a refuge, or a harbor
Where there is hope of safety. Funerals,
Wher'er I turn my frightened eyes, appall;
The temples groan with coffins, and the proud
And humble lie alike in lack of honor.

---

(4) *Il Rinascimento francese: studi e ricerche* (Turin: Società Editrice Internazionale, 1961), pp. 177-211. The fifth chapter of this work, «La fortuna del Petrarca in Francia nella prima metà del Cinquecento,» which treats the reception in France of all of Petrarch's works except the *Canzoniere*, is reprinted from *GSLI*, 127 (1950), 1-59.

(5) In *The Waning of the Middle Ages* (Garden City: Doubleday, 1954), p. 325, Johan Huizinga cautions: «As to Petrarch himself, we are always inclined to exaggerate the modern element in his mind and work ... Nothing is further from the truth. He is most emphatically a man of his time. The themes of which he treated were

The end of life presses upon my mind,
And I recall the dear ones I have lost,
Their cherished words, their faces, vanished now,
The consecrated ground is all too small
To hold the instant multitude of graves... (6)

Petrarch's intense anxiety and grief stemming from this experience never leave him completely. Twenty years later, in «Standomi un giorno,» the emotion is recollected in the tranquility of the poet's maturity but its force is poignantly renewed. «Standomi un giorno» deals with death and mutability, constant preoccupations of his mind and of his times, and a preoccupation of the poets to whom *canzone* 323 later appealed. In medieval poetry, an obsession with death appears in both religious and secular works; Huizinga treats this «vision of death» as characteristic of medieval European culture, permeating both the life and the art of the times. (7)

The uncertainty Petrarch expresses in his letter is part of the general state of insecurity, seen by Marc Bloch as the late medieval norm. It «made people's minds constantly and almost morbidly attentive to all manner of signs, dreams or hallucinations.» (8) Dreams had a special appeal, as always, and were discussed by theologians like St. Thomas, by *savants* like Albertus Magnus, and by poets like Petrarch. (9) Scholars even devised systems of dream classification which converged

---

those of the Middle Ages: *De contemptu mundi, De otio religiosorum, De vita solitaria.*»

(6) Quoted by Ernest Hatch Wilkins in *Life of Petrarch* (Chicago: Univ. of Chicago Press, 1963), pp. 79-80. This letter is one of the *Epistolae metricae* and is entitled *Ad se ipsum.*

(7) *The Waning of the Middle Ages,* pp. 138-151. Besides Huizinga's study, there have been many works on this and related subjects. See Edelgard Dubruck, *The Theme of Death in French Poetry of the Middle Ages and the Renaissance* (The Hague: Mouton, 1964), who covers much of the bibliography on the subject.

(8) Marc Bloch, *Feudal Society,* trans. L. A. Manyon (Chicago: Univ. of Chicago Press, 1961), I, 73.

(9) Lynn Thorndike, *A History of Magic and Experimental Science* (New York: Macmillan, 1929), II, 290-302.

and became stable by Petrarch's day. (10) Besides much theoretical material on occult happenings, there were, of course, numerous literary examples of the visionary technique, dating from classical antiquity. Petrarch had become acquainted with the literary usefulness of dreams in his favorite Latin authors, Cicero, who wrote a treatise on divination and the *Dream of Scipio,* and Virgil, who used dreams in his epic. Petrarch's poetic use of dreams and visions both reflects the popular fascination with the occult and continues a venerable literary motif. (11)

Although Petrarch disdained superstition (12) and espoused reason as the proper measure of things, (13) he was still caught up in the current of interest in the supernatural. While in some of his letters he recounts dreams of his own which he considered truly significant, Petrarch had concluded that dreams have a direct connection only with one's hopes and fears and do not necessarily predict or shape the future. (14) Accordingly, Petrarch uses the dream or visionary structure, in the *Trionfi* and in the second half of the *Canzoniere,* as a graphic means of poetic expression.

Petrarch may of course have chosen to use the dream in

---

(10) The most generally accepted system of dream classification, discussed at some length by Constance B. Hieatt in her study *The Realism of Dream Visions: The Poetic Exploitation of the Dream-Experience in Chaucer and his Contemporaries* (The Hague: Mouton, 1967), pp. 23-33, had five gradations: *insomnium, visium, somnium, oraculum,* and *visio.* The latter type is a waking vision.

(11) See *Studies of the Dream as a Technical Device in the Latin Epic and Drama* (Lancaster: Lancaster Press, 1927), Introduction (n. p.), where J. B. Stearns mentions no less than twenty-six handbooks on the interpretation of dreams from classical times, none of which are now extant.

(12) *A History of Magic and Experimental Science,* III, 217-222.

(13) In a letter to Boccaccio, Petrarch casts doubt on the veracity of prophecy. This letter is in *Epistolae seniles* (I, 5); it is translated by Morris Bishop in *Letters from Petrarch* (Bloomington: Indiana Univ. Press, 1966), pp. 225-228, and is discussed by Wilkins, *Life of Petrarch,* p. 183.

(14) Bishop, *Letters from Petrarch,* pp. 60-61 (*Epistolae familiares,* V, 7).

his poetry because he was always conscious of continuing a classical and a medieval literary tradition. He may have been indebted to his immediate predecessor Dante, in whose *Vita nuova,* for example, we find several dream visions woven into the poet's monologue, an examination of his *innamoramento* and its aftereffects. (15) The dream visions in sections III and XII are prophetic of future events, occur when the dreamer is asleep, and are described and explained in the *ragione.* While such manifestations resemble those in the *Trionfi* and certain other *Rime,* they differ from the vision in *canzone* 323. The vision in the sonnet of section IX of the *Vita nuova* is another matter. In this vision of the pilgrim *Amore,* who comes to him during a journey away from Beatrice, Dante dramatizes his own feelings of loss and subsequent grief. He indicates in the *ragione* that this poem is a waking vision; it seems to be, in fact, the projection or externalization of his own feelings and worries. (16)

The procedure in Dante's sonnet may have prompted Petrarch's use of the vision as a poetic device, but we may also find antecedents to Petrarch's visionary *canzone* in his own earlier works, especially the *Trionfi.* These poems tell of a poet's journey to the other world (again echoing Dante), where he meets famous people of both ancient and modern times whose loves and virtues, while subject to death and the ravages of time, are apt to win fame or the ultimate goal of eternity in a timeless heaven. Inspired by descriptions of the triumphal processions of ancient Rome, their vivid, pictorial character made them a favorite work of medieval and early Renaissance poets and artists. (17) The *Trionfi* were involved

---

(15) For an examination of this relationship, see Aldo S. Bernardo, «Petrarch's Attitude toward Dante,» *PMLA,* 70 (1955), 488-517.

(16) Dante explains: «E però lo dolcissimo segnore, lo quale mi segnoreggiava per la vertù de la gentilissima donna, ne la mia imaginazione apparve come peregrino leggeramente vestito e di vili drappi.» I cite from *La Vita nuova,* ed. Natalino Sapegno (Florence: Vallecchi, 1931), p. 51.

(17) For an examination of this aspect of Petrarchism, see

in the transportation of the visionary *canzone* abroad, and they also set something of a precedent in technique.

In the triumphs of love, chastity, and fame, the significance of the triumphal procession grows out of the analogical or associational mode of presentation which will be used in *canzone* 323. Throughout each procession the dreamer sees persons, historical symbols, gathered from ancient history, mythology, legend, and the Bible who are representative of the various earthly manifestations of love, chastity, and fame. The sight of Phaedra, Jaufré Rudel, Judith, Plato, and Alexander is intended to bring the stories of their actions or thoughts to bear upon the reader's impression and understanding of those qualities they exemplify. The impressive visual and pictorial nature of these processions as well as their moralistic themes made them the inspiration for painters and other artists and is brought to the reader's attention at the end of the *Trionfo d'amore* when the dreamer who sees the pageant compares himself to a man gazing back at a lengthy painting:

Rimirando er'io fatto al sol di neve
tanti spirti e sí chiari in carcer tetro
quasi lunga pittura in tempo breve,
che 'l pie' va innanzi, e l'occhio torna a dietro. (18)
(lines 163-166)

«Standomi un giorno» has been associated with the *Trionfi* by the critics. In an early essay, Francesco Pasqualigo argues

Robert Coogan, «Petrarch's *Trionfi* and the English Renaissance,» *SP*, 67 (1970), 306-327; Franco Simone, *Il Rinascimento francese*, pp. 177-211; Victor Massena, Prince d'Essling, and Eugene Müntz, *Pétrarque, ses études d'art, son influence sur les artistes, ses portraits, et ceux de Laure* (Paris: Gazette des beaux-arts, 1902); D. D. Carnicelli, *Lord Morley's Tryumphes of Fraunces Petrarcke: The First English Translation of the Trionfi* (Cambridge: Harvard Univ. Press, 1971), pp. 28-70.

(18) Francesco Petrarca, *Trionfi*, ed. Carlo Calcaterra (Turin: UTET, 1927), p. 63. All quotations from the *Trionfi* will be taken

that each of the six visions corresponds to one of the six triumphs, all of which are actually concerned with the death of Laura. (19) While we need not agree completely with Pasqualigo's thesis, it is possible to see the thematic and stylistic rapport between the two works. The succession of six graphic images in the *canzone* is a version of the processional technique of the longer work. And both *canzone* 323 and the *Trionfi* are visionary. The *Trionfo d'amore,* a work of the poet's early years, serves as an introduction to all the triumphs and is presented as a dream. The procession of famous lovers comes to the dreamer after he has fallen asleep on the grass:

> Ivi fra l'erbe, già del pianger fioco,
>   vinto dal sonno, *vidi* una gran luce,
>   e dentro assai dolor con breve gioco.
> *Vidi* un vittorioso e sommo duce,
>   pur com'un di color che 'n Campidoglio
>   trionfal carro a gran gloria conduce.
> I', che gioir di tal *vista* non soglio
>   per lo secol noioso in ch'i' mi trovo,
>   vòto d'ogni valor, pien d'ogn'orgoglio
> l'abito *in vista* sí leggiadro e novo
>   *mirai,* alzando *gli occhi* gravi e stanchi,
>   ch'altro diletto che 'mparar non provo:
>   (lines 10-21)

The visual character of his experience is announced by the verbs and nouns. Another early poem, Eclogue X, «Laurea Occidens,» of the *Bucolicum Carmen,* stresses the visionary aspect of his experience with the same repetition of the Latin

---

from this edition and will be cited in this study by line number. Italics are my own.

(19) *Le visioni del Petrarca nella canzone «Standomi un giorno» confrontate coi «Trionfi» dello stesso* (Rome: Bonghi, 1887). This argument has been rejected by Francesco Maggini, «La canzone delle visioni,» SPet, 1 (1948), 39.

vidi. (20) Interestingly enough, these visionary experiences often occur in pastoral settings like those of «Standomi un giorno.»

Antecedents of «Standomi un giorno» (a late poem, begun on October 13, 1368) can be found in the *Canzoniere* as well. Several dream poems display Laura appearing to the poet and addressing him in the tender terms she never used in life. The dream element appears in «Qual paura ho quando mi torna a mente» [249], in «O misera et orribil visïone» [251], where the poet explains the effect of past dreams on his emotions, and in «Quando il soave mio fido conforto» [359], where the poet shows Laura's displeasure over his lamenting. All these poems explain the past or some aspect of the lover's behavior but none are composed of a series of little pictures. Mario Praz claims that the procession of images in «Standomi un giorno» is actually similar to those in «Nel dolce tempo de la prima etade» [23] and in «Qual piú diversa e nova» [135]. (21) In the latter *canzone*, Petrarch takes the figures of comparison from medieval lapidaries and bestiaries as well as the ancient natural histories. (22) Petrarch compares himself or the lady to a series of strange and unusual things, always drawing from the comparison some explanatory statement about his love: he compares the lover to the phoenix, to the fountain of the sun, and to the two fountains on Fortune's island; the lady is compared to a magnet, a *catoblepas,* and to the spring of Epirus.

In «Nel dolce tempo» the lover undergoes six metamor-

---

(20) See Thomas G. Bergin, *Petrarch's Bucolicum Carmen* (New Haven: Yale Univ. Press, 1974), pp. 140-183 (especially lines 64-174), for both the Latin and English versions of this eclogue.

(21) «Petrarca e gli emblematisti» in *Ricerche anglo-italiane* (Rome: Istituto grafico Tiberino, 1944), pp. 306-307.

(22) *Ibid.,* p. 307. Praz notes: «In *Qual più diversa e nova* non è più in Ovidio, ma nei lapidari, nei bestiari, e nei *mirabilia* medievali che Petrarca cerca materia d'emblemi.» Petrarch's editors, Chiòrboli and Carducci, cite specific possibilities for the sources of the images in *canzone* 323, such as Pliny, Lucretius, St. Augustine, and Albertus Magnus.

phoses as a consequence of his lady's displeasure. Although these changes do not constitute an entire narrative like Ovid's, their meaning is enhanced and expanded by the allusions to Ovid's stories. Disturbed by his lady's unrelenting attitude, the lover turns into a laurel, an inversion of Ovid's tale of Apollo and Daphne; his hope destroyed, he laments his sorrow like Cycnus in the form of a swan; after stealing his heart, the lady swears him to a secrecy he cannot keep and like Battus, he is changed into a stone; when he admits his need for her, the lady leaves him transformed into a spring of tears like Byblis; like Echo deprived of her form, he remains only as bones and the vestige of a voice; finally, the lady—like Diana—avenges herself on him, changing him into a stag pursued by his own hounds. Robert Durling claims that *canzone* 323 develops the theme of metamorphosis which recurs in the *Canzoniere* and that the six metamorphoses in *canzone* 23 occur in three cycles whose rhythm is as follows:

> the lover loves, declares his love, and is repulsed and mourns in poetry ... The metamorphoses of Laura, presented in 323 are also six; and they echo the events of 23 and also 135, which describes the lover and the lady as six marvels of the world. ... Within the *Canzoniere* as a whole, it [323] balances 23, the canzone of the lover's mutability, and casts ironic light back on it and on 135. (23)

Still, this does not give us an exact idea of the poet's method

---

(23) *The Figure of the Poet in the Renaissance Epic* (Cambridge: Harvard Univ. Press, 1965), p. 83. For a detailed analysis of such transformations in the *Canzoniere*, see Marga Cottino-Jones, «The Myth of Apollo and Daphne in Petrarch's *Canzoniere*: The Dynamics and Literary Function of Transformation» in Aldo Scaglione, ed., *Francis Petrarch*, pp. 152-176; a detailed analysis of *canzone* 23 can be found in Dennis Dutschke, «The Textual Situation and Chronological Assessment of Petrarch's *Canzone* XXIII,» *Italian Quarterly* 18 (1974), 37-69.

in «Standomi un giorno,» because the catastrophes are not truly metamorphoses.

The individual images in «Standomi un giorno» can be traced to some of the same sources as those used in «Nel dolce tempo» and «Qual piú diversa e nova.» However, unlike the metamorphoses of Ovid, or the changes in these other two *canzoni,* the reversals that occur in «Standomi un giorno» do not involve a change from one form of life to another. The change they suffer is one of the highest seriousness: they relate to the consequences of Laura's death and imply something about the nature of human frailty and the universal power of mutability.

The highly pictorial images in «Standomi un giorno,» which result in part from the requirements of a vision, reveal both its relation to and its differences from other Petrarchan compositions. The beast, the ship, the fountain, the laurel, the phoenix, and the lady occur throughout the *Rime* and elsewhere, but in this instance they are presented in a somewhat different manner, which modifies the usual relationship to the psychological state of the lover. In brief, the poem belongs in a tradition; we shall discover, in the succeeding chapters, wherein it differs from the vision poetry that preceded it and from Petrarch's other Italian poems, as well as some reasons for its wide-spread popularity during the Renaissance.

CHAPTER II

PETRARCH AS VISIONARY

A lesser known facet of Petrarch's enormous influence is his stance as a visionary in *canzone* 323, «Standomi un giorno solo a la fenestra.» The poem supposedly describes an occasion when the poet, reflecting on the death of Laura and what it meant to him, was granted a six-fold vision which offered him graphic emblematic illustrations of his sorrow. It was Petrarch's belief that the poet's imagination sets forth psychological, moral, and historical truths under the veil of fictions. (1) Hence, his fiction that he is standing and looking out a window:

> Standomi un giorno solo a la fenestra,
> Onde cose vedea tante e sí nove
> Ch'era sol di mirar quasi già stanco,
> (lines 1-3)

The pretense that these are real events being recorded from memory lends another dimension of immediacy and reality to the poetry. Subsequently, the poet stresses the idea of

---

(1) Petrarch thus defines the nature and function of poetry in «The Coronation Oration,» trans. Ernest Hatch Wilkins, in his *Studies in the Life and Works of Petrarch* (Cambridge: Medieval Academy of America, 1955), p. 307.

seeing to give his fiction a vivid, concrete foundation and to increase the impact of the observations upon the reader. An allusion to memory in the middle of the poem («E sol de la memoria mi sgomento,» line 48) reminds the reader how great a power past events have on the emotions. (2) The *congedo* specifically states that the *canzone* is made up of six visions, sights witnessed:

> Canzon, tu puoi ben dire:
> —Queste sei visïoni al signor mio
> Han fatto un dolce di morir desio.—
>   (lines 73-75)

Although the visionary aspect of *canzone* 323 is almost unique within the *Canzoniere,* it easily conforms to Petrarch's habitual mode of thought which is pictorial and analogical. The small pageant of figures which pass before the visionary's eyes calls to mind the elaborate pageantry of the *Trionfi.* At first the six scenes with their images of differing origins seem disconnected. This impression is dispelled as we recognize the associational organization common to the processions of vivid images in dreams. These visions are not technically dreams, but they evince several phantasmagoric traits. In a dream there is a free, undeterminable, unlocalized setting. In the poem, the background for each vision is vague and generalized. Petrarch mentions only briefly a direction or a place: «un boschetto novo,» «quel medesmo bosco,» «da man destra,» «la selva,» «alto mar.» Each situation evokes an appropriate setting which is vividly present for one moment and then abruptly and mysteriously disappears. The poem resembles a dream as well in its freedom from the limitations of time and

---

(2) In *Petrarch* (New York: Twayne, 1970), p. 169, Thomas G. Bergin points out that «the eternal impact of the *Canzoniere,* whether we think of it as a source of literary influence or in the sense of the reader's response, is the remorselessness of time and the sad and yet somehow consoling uses of memory.»

space, in the suppression of narrative continuity, and in the absence of explanations.

United structurally by the fiction of the spectator at the window, the *canzone* is divided into six stanzas and a *congedo,* each stanza of twelve lines containing one precipitous and dramatic event. While Fredi Chiappelli's judgment that the reactions of the witness give the poem its essential energy is understandable, it is equally justifiable to say that the central image in each stanza is what first engages the reader's attention and what gives the poem its dramatic force. (3) There is a minimum of self-analysis in this *canzone*. Instead of trying to make us understand his emotions, the poet tries to make us see, through his poetic narrative, why his reactions are what they are.

Each of the six images in *canzone* 323 is dealt a tragic blow. Because the images of the beast, the ship, the fountain, the laurel, the phoenix, and the lady are the most exquisite creatures in the milieu of the *Canzoniere,* (4) the emotional impact of their destruction is so forceful that they dominate the reader's perception of the poetry. It is precisely the formal characteristics of these images which have called forth the varying descriptions of the style of the poem. The figures have been referred to as metamorphoses, emblems, medallions on a necklace, examples of *ekphrasis*. We have already pointed out that the events in the poem are not really metamorphoses. (5) Not change from one physical state to another but destruction and catastrophe are the theme of the poem.

Chiappelli observes that the poem has «poche analogie nel *Canzoniere*, se pur gli si possano apparentare parecchi

---

(3) Fredi Chiappelli, *Studi sul linguaggio del Petrarca*: *La canzone delle visioni* (Florence: Olschki, 1971), p. 28.

(4) These are major images in several poems in the *Canzoniere*: the *fera* in 135 and 152; the ship in 26, 189, and 235; the laurel in 23, 29, and 337; the fountain in 23 and 135; and the phoenix in 185, 210, and 321.

(5) Durling, *The Figure of the Poet*, p. 83.

casi.» (6) He adds that the work is a variation on the theme of mutability having a «struttura a collana di medaglioni»; (7) this implies a *rapprochement* between the poet's and the engraver's craft as well as the essential unity of the disparate images. Petrarch's graphic metaphors prompt Mario Praz to say that «Standomi un giorno» is an example of *ekphrasis* and that «every stanza of 'Standomi un giorno' needs only a figure to become an emblem proper.» (8) These comments help to define the essential quality of the visionary style. The comparison of Petrarch's technique with *ekphrasis* and emblematics is related both to the history of the poem's influence and to its graphic liveliness, a striking illustration of the Horatian dictum *ut pictura poesis*. (9) While Petrarch never goes to the extent of creating poetic metaphors out of the terminology of sculpture and painting as Michelangelo later does, (10) this poetry has definite affinities with the visual arts, which likewise depend upon the spectator's ability to translate the visible into the intelligible after thoughtful meditation.

Each stanza is organized in the same manner. Structural repetition increases the impact of each successive catastrophe. In his study of the variants, Fredi Chiappelli finds a tertiary subdivision in the individual stanzas: the appearance of the miraculous figure against an appropriate background impresses the witness; the intervention of a destructive force brings about the death of the figure; the witness laments in terror and grief. (11) But Praz notes that «ogni stanza è interamente occupata dalla descrizione del simbolo, sottointeso è il referi-

---

(6) «La canzone delle visioni e il sostrato tematico della 'fabula inexpleta',» *GSLI*, 141 (1964), 321.

(7) *Ibid.*

(8) *Studies in Seventeenth-Century Imagery* (Rome: Edizioni di Storia e Letteratura, 1964), p. 13.

(9) See Praz, *Ricerche anglo-italiane*, p. 305.

(10) This technique is discussed by C. B. Beall in «The Literary Figure of Michelangelo,» *Italica*, 41 (1964), 235-251, and by Glauco Cambon in «Sculptural Form as Metaphysical Conceit in Michelangelo's Verse,» *SR*, 70 (1962), 155-163.

(11) *Studi sul linguaggio del Petrarca*, p. 28. For a more recent

mento al caso personale del poeta.» (12) Since the major portion of each stanza is devoted to the central image, we shall first examine the genesis and development of these images, later exploited pictorially in the woodcuts of Jan van der Noot's *Theatre*. In addition, we shall examine Petrarch's adaptation of the visionary method to give an objective yet intensely emotional account of his *innamoramento* and subsequent bereavement. Memory has turned this experience into an abstract presentation of beauty doomed to destruction. The reader witnesses the spectacle with the poet but his tears are the Virgilian *lacrimae rerum*. For the reader, the spectacle has another dimension, because he observes the reactions of the *persona* which spring from a personal involvement.

Because of the visionary framework, the concreteness and formal beauty of the central images are requisite. However, the physical delineation of the six images is not specific in the modern sense. The medieval or Renaissance poet was motivated by the criteria of decorum and significance and thought that «art should find the intelligible in the visible.» (13) A vision of this sort must be concrete, but it is also revelatory. Petrarch remains faithful to his visionary framework, and his images are both concrete and suggestive. The descriptive words are sufficiently colorful while, at the same time, they point to the essential worth of the thing described. (14) The poem is a metaphoric recreation of Petrarch's love

---

treatment of the structure of *canzone* 323, see Fredi Chiappelli, «An Analysis of Structuration in Petrarch's Poetry» in Aldo Scaglione, ed., *Francis Petrarch*, pp. 105-116.

(12) *Ricerche anglo-italiane*, p. 307.

(13) For a discussion of the criteria of decorum and significance to which this chapter is indebted, see Rosemund Tuve, *Elizabethan and Metaphysical Imagery: Renaissance Poetic and Twentieth-Century Critics* (Chicago: Univ. of Chicago Press, 1947), p. 53.

(14) In his introduction to *An Anthology of Spanish Poetry 1500-1700: Part I*, 1500-1580 (Oxford: Oxford Univ. Press, 1965), p. xxiii, Arthur Terry explains that in Renaissance poetry, «images ... are used to direct the reader's mind towards the value of what is described, rather than to its precise physical appearance.» Terry's discussion follows Tuve's more detailed treatment.

affair and the images, which are metaphors for Laura, his lady and muse, are set forth as the treasures of Petrarch's poetic experience.

The beast, ship, laurel, fountain, phoenix and lady derive from classical sources and appear frequently in the *Canzoniere*. Yet, within this vision, Petrarch reuses them in an original way, recording the uniqueness of his lady and his experience. This *fera* is still the elusive creature slightly beyond his reach, but here the barrier is death, the final separation. Other vessels in the *Rime* stand as metaphors for the poet's tormented soul, but this *nave* is transformed into an extravagant image of Laura whose destruction marks the loss of the poet's most cherished treasure. The last four images of Laura are classical or mythical, but their legends are also modified. The pastoral harmony and idyllic beauty of the laurel and the fountain cannot withstand the rigors of the finite world. A cataclysm unexpectedly swallows up the fountain, a *locus amoenus* which recalls the exquisite creations of Ovid and Horace. (15) The plant traditionally immune to lightning, the laurel, is uprooted by a sudden flash from the heavens. (16) By the fifth stanza, the emotion of surprise turns to despair. At the climax of the poem, the immortal phoenix, beholding the destruction of the laurel and the fountain, without the usual cycle of burning and regeneration, strikes itself down with its own beak. When the latter-day Euridice of the final vision is bitten on the heel (not on the ankle) by a small snake, there remains no pos-

---

(15) Maggini, pp. 44-45, makes the comparison between Petrarch's fountain and those of Horace and Ovid, noting that the language in this stanza is highly polished. It is perhaps in this respect that Petrarch is most classical. As Pierre de Nolhac points out in *Pétrarque et l'humanisme* (Paris: Champion, 1907), I, 11: «Ce qui l'a séduit dans la littérature antique c'est le caractère d'oeuvre d'art.»

(16) Petrarch discusses the traditional qualities attributed to the laurel in «The Coronation Oration,» trans. by Wilkins in *Studies in the Life and Works of Petrarch*, p. 312. For another instance in Petrarch's poetry where the destruction of the laurel by lightning occurs, the visionary Eclogue X, see Thomas G. Bergin, *Petrarch's Bucolicum Carmen*, pp. 140-183.

sibility for her poet-lover to retrieve her from the land of the dead.

Traditionally, these six visions have been interpreted as an allegory of Laura's death, and the early commentators have tried to see references to Laura in the descriptive elements of the poem. Sometimes their insistence on the significance of certain details offends logic; however, it reveals their understanding of the personal nature of the vision. On the whole, Petrarch's method is to make us associate the image with the Laura of the other poems, and thus to create metaphors of which one term is only implied. The complex of detail in each vision speaks of much more than Laura's death; it also reveals something of her beauty, her life, and her spirituality. Evoking the figure of a woman with such adjectives as *umana,* Petrarch alludes to a burial with the phrase «chiusa in un sasso,» and more directly to the plague in which Laura died with the reference to a *tempesta orïental.* The careful framing of the individual images heightens the emotional impact of their destruction precisely because so many of the details recall the Laura of the *Rime* in her varying attitudes. The poet, who wants us to imagine Laura in all her grace, selects modifiers which suggest her physical beauty and its value to her lover (*bella, giovenetto, schietto, oro, porporo, ebeno, neve*). Other modifiers pertain especially to her spiritual qualities (*onesta, lieta, felice, santi, celeste*). Further, some of the vocabulary is reminiscent of the *stilnovisti* (*bella donna, pietate, gentil, leggiadra*), and evokes the relationship of the poet-lover and his *donna angelicata* with her transcendental qualities.

The careful delineation of the central images reflects that association of painting and poetry made by Renaissance critics and must have contributed to De Sanctis' judgment of the world of the *Rime* as «questo bel mondo plastico.» (17) But the variety in «Standomi un giorno» is not limited to the central images; it is the goal of every detail in the poem. This

----

(17) Francesco De Sanctis, *Saggio critico sul Petrarca* (Naples: A. Morano, 1932), p. 253.

extraordinary workmanship is Chiappelli's real subject, and he attempts to show that each word and each sound are motivated by Petrarch's attention to detail and by his consciousness of the musical possibilities of verse. (18) Maggini remarks that the description of the fountain in stanza four is one of the most corrected in the manuscripts of the *Rime* and that Petrarch's critical self-conscious search for perfection of form and style looks toward the «classicism» of the Renaissance:

> Abbiamo visto elementi di allegoria e
> di figure che ci riportano al pensiero
> del medio evo e potrebbero ricorrere
> negli scrittori dei secoli precedenti;
> ma anche un modo di trattarli (che per
> l'arte è tutto) che annunzia un altro
> senso della poesia, un desiderio di
> forme armoniose, una squisita eleganza
> espressiva, insomma tutti i caratteri
> che distinguono il Rinascimento. (19)

The variants bring to light Petrarch's humanistic belief in the power of the word and his concern for linguistic perfection. After the second stanza, Petrarch strives to avoid the verbs of sight and to suppress temporal conjunctions which mark the progress of his vision. On the linguistic level, he searches for variety in word and sound, accentuating always the unique qualities of his central images. The last four sketches show the poet constantly pruning away prosaic phrases and repetitions. When Petrarch uses the modifier «gold» in several stanzas, he calls attention to the exceptional value of his

---

(18) See Chiappelli, *Studi sul linguaggio del Petrarca* as well as E. H. Wilkins, *The Making of the «Canzoniere» and Other Petrarchan Studies* (Rome: Edizione di Storia e Letteratura, 1951), and Ruth S. Phelps, *The Earlier and Later Forms of Petrarch's Canzoniere* (Chicago: Univ. of Chicago Press, 1925).
(19) Maggini, p. 50.

creations. On the syntactic level, the poem is a combination of classical periods (20) and paratactic phrases which contribute to the smooth rhythm of the vision and which emphasize the spectator's outbursts. All these refinements in style show how Petrarch enriches and enriches and makes the things lost splendid and precious, shining and invaluable. This is, of course, more than praise of Laura's remarkable fairness; it is a statement of how dear Laura and now her memory are to him.

Petrarch's craftsmanship is never simply art for art's sake. All of the stylistic resources of the poet are directed toward revealing something of the nature of love and its implications in the earthly sphere. The poet wants us to feel the power of Laura's influence in his life and to realize that the onlooker is a vital part of the visionary poem. Certainly the deliberate shadings of the expressions of sorrow indicate the poet's interest in the psychology of the witness at the window. Praz feels that Petrarch conceals autobiographical facts behind images or myths as he writes of Laura's death in «Standomi un giorno,» (21) and Chiappelli believes that the poet is less concerned with his configuration of Laura's death than with his own emotional reaction. The latter contends that it is really the poet-spectator who is most revealed in his precipitous fall from ecstasy to dismay:

> ... il punto critico è la caduta precipitosa, inattesa, inarrestabile, dall'estasi allo sgomento: il vero avvenimento non è nella scena, è nello spirito. (22)

Chiappelli may exaggerate the development of emotion in the speaker, although we can discern some progression from his

---

(20) Maggini, p. 41, emphasizes the long periods in «Standomi un giorno,» such as that which encloses the entire sketch of the *fera*.
(21) *Ricerche anglo-italiane*, p. 309.
(22) *Studi sul linguaggio del Petrarca*, p. 29.

conclusions that all things die and that nothing but sorrow is lasting to his expression of a wish for death. Still, Chiappelli calls attention to that portion of the poetry which is over-shadowed by the brilliance of the images.

Elsewhere Petrarch is more analytic in his approach, appeal-ing more to the reader's intellect. In «Standomi un giorno,» on the other hand, he wants the reader to exalt in his lady's inspirational beauty and to grieve with him at her death. The spectacle, always presented in a sympathetic manner, elicits awe, respect, appreciation, and a judgment from its audience. The things destroyed have a special nobility («la fera gentil»), moral superiority («ricca merce onesta»), youth and purity («un lauro giovenetto e schietto»), exquisite beauty and even divinity («forma celeste et immortale»). The visionary, overcome by the beauty and harmony of the sights, is lulled into a kind of religious rapture. Yet, each time his almost mystical experience terminates not in the sublime but in the harsh world of reality and mutability. With each vision, the expectations of the spectators are disappointed, and with each vision, the witness at the window goes from a state of passive bliss to a state of passive shock. He can do no more than stand there and vent his distress in the little maxims which punctuate each stanza. By the fifth vision, he has begun to expect the tragic destruction and comments upon the mutability of all things immediately preceding the suicide of the phoenix.

Although the idea that mutability respects neither beauty, youth nor goodness is repeated stanza after stanza, Petrarch attempts to achieve some variety in the spectator's feelings. Chiappelli stresses this aspect of the poem, finding a new movement in the poetry after the first two stanzas because the sensory awareness of the *persona* expands to both sight and sound and because the objective viewpoint supposedly maintained throughout the first two stanzas gives way to a realization of personal involvement in the little tragedies. (23)

---

(23) *Ibid.*, pp. 202-203. Maggini, p. 39, on the other hand, sees

The onlooker makes his involvement personal when he places himself at the window. Also, the death of the *fera* «chiusa in un sasso» makes him grieve («E *mi* fe' sospirar sua dura sorte»). After a suppression of the *persona* in the second stanza, with the destruction of the mythical ship, the speaker again stresses his presence by picturing himself looking at the laurel tree just before it is uprooted: «E mirando 'l *io* fiso.» Speaking of the effect of the catastrophe, he makes a direct reference to his own life: «onde *mia* vita è trista, / Ché simile ombra mai non si racquista.» At the sight of the definitive death of the phoenix, the pain is personal: «Onde 'l cor di pietate, e d'amor *m'*arse.» The pronominal construction stresses personal involvement throughout the *canzone*.

Some of the outbursts call attention to the spectator's distress directly; others do so only implicitly. Reversing the usual order of things, Petrarch elaborates commonplaces about earthly mutability to define his grief over Laura. The proverbial tone of «Ogni cosa al fin vola» (line 55), or «Ahi, nulla altro che pianto al mondo dura!» (line 72), conveys his consciousness of the universality of his personal affliction. As he had in «Chi vuol veder quantunque po Natura» [248], where he determines that «Cosa bella mortal, passa e non dura» (line 8), he concludes here that Laura must die because envious death steals away all the sooner that which is most beautiful. Hence, his images progress from the *fera* to the *bella donna,* a most explicit metaphor for Laura, or perhaps, as Maggini suggests, even Laura herself, who was in a special sense Petrarch's own Euridice. (24)

Petrarch, a modern Orpheus, loses his lady to death, but her memory continually inspires him. Although the poet's grief is intense, his artistic self-control allows him to maintain an attitude toward death which lacks bitterness and shows restraint. In Petrarch's works in general, there is neither

---

no development of concepts but only a constant return to the theme of Laura's death.

(24) Maggini, p. 47.

excessive fear of death, neither fanatical denunciation of the flesh nor complete absorption in spiritual matters. The balance in the tone and diction of the poetry prefigures that classical equilibrium which became a goal of the literary Renaissance. Death permeates the latter portion of the *Canzoniere,* but it is never horrible or ugly but somehow at times desirable. It has an attraction for the virtuous lady in the sixth vision of our *canzone* because it brings her to spiritual safety: dying, she is *lieta* and *secura,* consistent with the picture of the womanly Laura-Beatrice Thomas G. Bergin finds in this portion of the cycle. (25) Paradoxically, death, which has deprived the impassioned poet of his lady-muse and has shaped his grief, is also the object of his final desire in the poem. Even though grief is a fact of life to which the living poet cannot reconcile himself, his poetic expression never becomes either maudlin sentiment or unreasonable terror, perhaps because he now finds his own mortality cumbersome (unlike the true Orpheus), and like the lady, would seek his own spiritual satisfaction. This expression of the *liebestod* is epitomized in the antithetic and bittersweet «dolce di morir desio.»

This desire is not the emotion of a moment but a consequence of an act of memory (line 48). Recreating a remembered moment of his emotional life, this time a painful one, the poet presents it with fascination, with wonder (*novo, estranio*), with surprise (*subito, breve ora, in un punto*), with a sense of past and present, and by exteriorizing what is inward (like Dante with his pilgrim). It is his old inner treasure that is so rich a *merce* and an inspiration for his patient and passionate description of it. The loss itself has become as much a part of this as the discovery of love, and his despair is something he has grown accustomed to; it is inseparable from the total phenomenon and is a «*dolce* di morir desio.»

«Standomi un giorno» finds the poet a spectator, but that

---

(25) *Petrarch*, pp. 163-165; Bergin's view is based upon a distinction made by Carlo Calcaterra, *Nella selva del Petrarca* (Bologna: Cappelli, 1942), chapters 2 and 7.

which has become spectacle is complex, even though the images tend to simplify it all. The poet attempts to suggest the magnitude of his deprivation and his sorrow through a series of catastrophes which befall metaphorical images of Laura's perfection. This poem records the poet's idealized memory of Laura, his grief at her death, and his present attitude toward this often treated subject. Laura alive was an inestimable and unattainable treasure, his grief at her death was sharp and deep, but this sad experience has retreated into the past and the memory serves as an inexhaustible source of poetry, a present and attainable treasure. (26) The sorrow is now muted and the lament has become song. Laura's beauty is now generalized, more noble, almost superhuman, and expressed not as a girl remembered, but as an abstraction lodged in a impersonal metaphor. This visionary style and the internal pathos appealed to the Renaissance reader, if we are to believe Gabriel Harvey, (27) for the poetry speaks of love and the passage of time (28) and provides a means of representing personal emotion in less subjective, pictorial terms. Consolation for the sorrow born into earthly creations rests in our impression that through poetry and memory beauty can endure.

---

(26) In *Petrarch, Laura & the 'Triumphs'* (Albany: State Univ. of New York Press, 1974), p. 200, Aldo S. Bernardo suggests that Laura is ultimately «the spirit that inspires man's powers of *ben far* to the point of deserving *immortal bellezza* for their *eterna fama,*» an amalgam of the best of the classical and Christian traditions (see especially pp. 42, 200-201).

(27) *The Works of Gabriel Harvey,* ed. Alexander B. Grosart (1884; rpt. New York: AMS Press, 1966), I, 94, contains an interesting letter to Edmund Spenser: «I dare saye you wyll holde yourselfe reasonably wel satisfied, if youre *Dreames* be but as well esteemed of in Englande, as *Petrarches Visions* be in Italy: which I assure you, is the very worst I wish you.»

(28) Bergin, *Petrarch,* p. 169, remarks in this regard that the motif of passing time is another aspect of the muse of memory and that the acute awareness of this human condition is essentially new in Petrarch.

Chapter III

MAROT'S VISIONS: TRANSLATION AND A NEW POETIC IDIOM

DES VISIONS DE PETRARQUE

De Tuscan en françoys

Un jour estant seulet à la fenestre,
Vey tant de cas nouveaulx devant mes yeulx,
Que d'en tant veoir fasché me convint estre.
  Si m'apparut une bische à main dextre,
Belle pour plaire au souverain des dieux.
Chassée estoit de deux chiens envieux,
Un blanc, un noir, qui par mortel effort
La gente beste aux flans mordoient si fort,
Qu'au dernier pas en bref temps l'ont menée
Cheoir soubz un roc. Et là, la cruaulté
De mort vainquit une grande beauté,
Dont souspirer me feit sa destinée.

  Puis en mer haulte un navire advisoye,
Qui tout d'hebene et blanc yvoire estoit,
A voiles d'or et à cordes de soye;
Doulx fut le vent, la mer paisible et coye,
Le ciel par tout cler se manifestoit.
La belle nef pour sa charge portoit
Riches tresors; mais tempeste subite,
En troublant l'air, ceste mer tant irrite,

— 33 —

3

Que la nef heurte un roc caché soubz l'onde.
O grand' fortune: ô crevecueur trop gref,
De veoir perir en un moment si bref
La grand' richesse à nulle autre seconde!

Après je vey sortir divins rameaulx
D'un laurier jeune, en un nouveau boscage,
Et me sembla veoir un des arbriseaulx
De paradis, tant y avoit d'oyseaulx
Diversement chantans à son umbrage.
Ces grans delictz ravirent mon courage,
Et ayant l'oeil fiché sur ce laurier,
Le ciel entour commence à varier
Et à noircir, dont la fouldre grand' erre
Vint arracher celuy plant bien heureux,
Qui me faict estre à jamais langoureux,
Car plus telle umbre on ne recouvre en terre.

Au mesme boys sourdoit d'un vif rocher
Fontaine d'eau murmurant soefvement;
De ce lieu frais tant excellent et cher
N'osoient pasteurs ne bouviers approcher,
Mais mainte Muse et Nymphe seulement,
Qui de leurs voix accordoient doulcement
Au son de l'eau. Là j'assis mon desir,
Et lors que plus j'y prenois de plaisir,
Je vey, helas! de terre ouvrir un gouffre
Qui la fontaine et le lieu devora,
Dont le mien cueur grand regret encor a;
Et y pensant, du seul penser je souffre.

Au boys je vey un seul phenix portant
Aesles de pourpre, et le chef tout doré:
Estrange estoit, dont pensay en l'instant
Veoir quelque corps celeste, jusque à tant
Qu'il vint à l'arbre en pieces demouré,
Et au ruisseau que terre a devoré.

Que diray plus? Toute chose enfin passe:
Quand ce phenix veit les rameaux en place,
Le tronc rompu, l'eau sèche d'autre part,
Comme en desdaing, de son bec s'est feru,
Et des humains sur l'heure disparu,
Dont de pitié et d'amour mon cueur ard.

   Enfin je vey une dame si belle,
Qu'en y songeant tousjours je brusle et tremble:
Entre herbe et fleurs pensive marchoit elle,
Humble de soy, mais contre amour rebelle,
Et blanche cotte avoit, comme il me semble,
Faicte en tel art, que neige et or ensemble
Sembloient meslez; mais en sus la ceincture
Couverte estoit d'une grand' nue obscure,
Et au tallon un serpenteau la blesse,
Dont languissoit comme une fleur cueillie;
Puis asseurée en liesse est saillie.
Las! rien ne dure au monde que tristesse.

   O chanson mienne, en tes conclusions
Dy hardiment: Ces six grans visions
A mon seigneur donnent un doulx desir
De briefvement soubz la terre gesir. (1)

Petrarch's influence upon French literature had begun in
the late fourteenth and early fifteenth centuries, when he was
known primarily as a moralist and humanist. (2) However,
during the wars of the French in Italy, they became acquainted
with the Italian court poets popular at the time, through

---

(1) Clément Marot, *Oeuvres complètes de Clément Marot*, ed.
Abel Grenier (Paris: Garnier, n. d.), II, 144-146. Since C. A. Mayer's
sixth volume of the complete works of Marot, the volume containing
his translations, has not yet appeared, all quotations from Marot's
translation are taken from Grenier's edition and will be noted by
line number in the text. Italics are my own.
(2) Simone, *Il Rinascimento francese*, pp. 147, 175.

whom they came to know Petrarch as the lover of Laura. C. A. Mayer and D. Bentley-Cranch establish that Petrarchism is evident in the work of Jean Marot and becomes an integral part of the early work of his son Clément. (3) They also show that some of Clément Marot's *rondeaux*, which date from before 1527, draw their inspiration not only from Serafino, who had been at the court of Charles VIII, but from others of Petrarch's Italian followers, such as Olimpo di Sassoferrato, il Cariteo, and Bembo, who brought imitators back to the true spirit of the *Canzoniere*. (4)

C. A. Mayer, Marot's modern editor, explains that errors in literary history and prejudices of taste have prevented critics from recognizing the Petrarchan elements, thematic or stylistic, in Marot's early poems. (5) That he knew of Petrarch's *Canzoniere* quite early, there is no doubt. The *Temple de Cupido,* one of his first works, contains a reference to

---

(3) «Le premier pétrarquiste français: Jean Marot,» *BHR*, 27 (1965), 183-185. Mayer and Bentley-Cranch in «Clément Marot, poète pétrarquiste,» *BHR*, 28 (1966), 32, point out that since Clément followed his father's example in other matters, he probably learned his Petrarchism from him. See also E. M. Rutson, «A Note on Jean Marot's Debt to Italian Sources,» *MLR*, 61 (1966), 25-28. Margarita White, «Petrarchism in the French Rondeau before 1527,» *FS*, 22 (1968), 287-295, suggests that Petrarchism may have been even more widespread than research has so far shown.

(4) «Clément Marot, poète pétrarquiste,» pp. 32-51, especially pp. 32-33. These findings show Joseph Vianey's contention that there were no French imitators of Petrarch before Marot's exile in Ferrara to be incorrect. Vianey, pp. 43-44, finds one exception in Jean Lemaire de Belges. The title of his *Trois Comptes intitulez de Cupido et de Atropos* states that the first story «fut inventé par Seraphin poète italien.» It is perhaps true that Marot brought with him from his stay in Ferrara the form of the sonnet later adopted as the regular form in French. See C. A. Mayer, «Le premier sonnet français: Marot, Mellin de Saint-Gelais et Jean Bouchet,» *RHLF*, 67 (1967), 481. In a recent article, «L'Introduction du sonnet en France,» *RPh*, 26 (1972), 64, Marcel Françon has questioned some of Mayer's conclusions.

(5) «Clément Marot and Literary History» in *Studies in French Literature Presented to H. W. Lawton,* eds. J. C. Ireson, I. D. McFarlane, and Garnet Ross (New York: Barnes & Noble, 1968), pp. 247-260.

Petrarch's love poetry which suggests Marot's awareness of its authoritative reputation; he makes the *Canzoniere* one of the «holy» books in the religion of love:

> Ovidius, maistre Alain Charretier,
> Petrarche, aussi le Rommant de la Rose,
> Sont les Messelz, Breviaire & Psaultier,
> Qu'en ce sainct Temple on list, en Rime & Prose; (6)

It is among Marot's *rondeaux,* a medieval form renewed by the inclusion of Petrarchan themes and devices, that the Petrarchan influence is greatest. Marot is attracted to certain *concetti* and antitheses and writes of the unhappy lover who cherishes his unhappiness, of the unfortunate lover's solitude and sadness, of the lady's perfection and virtue, and of the passing of time. (7) These new thematic interests provide a motive for his later translations of «Standomi un giorno» and several sonnets.

After 1527, Marot's Petrarchism manifests itself somewhat less originally but perhaps more significantly for the future of French poetry. There is the «Chant-Royal dont le Roy bailla le Refrain,» written before 1531 and containing a refrain («Desbender l'Arc ne guerist point la Playe»), which is a translation of the last line of Petrarch's sonnet «Erano i capei d'oro a l'aura sparsi» [90]. (8) Some of his epigrams, a poetic form to which Sebillet compares the sonnet, (9) also show Petrarchan influence. (10) During this period, Marot translated

---

(6) Clément Marot, *Oeuvres lyriques,* ed. C. A. Mayer (London: Athlone Press, 1964), p. 103. Marot might only have been imitating Jean Lemaire who had mentioned Petrarch in his *Temple de Venus.*

(7) See Mayer and Bentley-Cranch, «Clément Marot, poète pétrarquiste,» pp. 36-43, and Clément Marot, *Oeuvres diverses,* ed. C. A. Mayer (London: Athlone Press, 1966), pp. 21-28.

(8) This date is cited by C. A. Mayer, «Les Oeuvres de Clément Marot: L'économie de l'édition critique,» *BHR,* 29 (1967), 359.

(9) Thomas Sebillet, *Art Poétique françoys,* ed. Félix Gaiffe (Paris: Droz, 1932), p. 115.

(10) Mayer and Bentley-Cranch, «Clément Marot, poète pétrar-

«Standomi in giorno,» which appeared among the *Chantz divers* in the editions of the *Suite de l'Adolescence Clementine,* published in 1533 and 1534, with the title «Le Chant des visions de Petrarque.» (11) Finally, before 1542, Marot wrote three original sonnets and translated six others, mainly from the second half of the *Canzoniere.* (12) Among the sonnets translated by Marot are «Chi vuol veder» [352], which laments the beauty which endures but briefly, and «Lasciato hai, Morte» [338], which describes how Laura's death has deprived the world of its sun. Another two, «Li angeli eletti» [346] and «Da' piú belli occhi» [348], significantly deal with the Laura-Beatrice who has taken her place among the blessed in heaven. Thus, Marot, a poet noted for his wit and light-heartedness, shows a consistent interest in the somber and more serious aspects of Petrarch's love poems. These translations are clearly related to the matter of «Standomi un giorno.»

V. L. Saulnier points out that Francis I appreciated Petrarch and may have requested that Marot translate some of the Italian poet's work. Saulnier claims, in fact, that the translation of «Standomi un giorno» was done at the king's command. (13) Whatever his motivation, Marot was the first

---

quiste,» pp. 47-50, claim that the problem of Petrarchan inspiration in the *Epigrammes* is complex.

(11) Mayer, «Les Oeuvres de Clément Marot: L'économie de l'édition critique,» p. 359. Without Mayer's edition of Marot's translations, it has been difficult to date this poem or to furnish a good text.

(12) According to Pierre Villey, *Marot et Rabelais* (Paris: Champion, 1923), pp. 339-397, Marot's translations of Petrarch's sonnets were done before November 1542. C. A. Mayer, «Le premier sonnet français,» p. 481, dates the three original sonnets between the summer of 1536 and the summer of 1538.

(13) *Les Elégies de Clément Marot* (Paris: Société d'édition d'enseignement supérieur, 1968), pp. 173-179. See also Alan Boase, *The Poetry of France* (London: Methuen, 1952), p. xli, who says: «Humanist and Italian influence on him was quite negligible. If he translated the third *canzone* and some six of Petrarch's sonnets and thus ranks with Mellin as the first to use the form in France, it was at the King's express invitation.»

outside Italy to translate Petrarch's visionary *canzone*. (14) Marot's successes in general were not accidental, for he was conscious of his milieu and aware of what he was doing artistically. (15) His careful cultivation of genres, one of his main preoccupations in this period of experimentation, is part of his effort to revive French poetry by introducing classical forms. (16) What better example to imitate than Petrarch, who was well enough known that Sebillet could refer to him as «le prince dés Poétes Italiens, duquel l'archétype dés Sonnetz a esté tiré.» (17)

From the beginning of his career, when he put Virgil's first eclogue into French, Marot understands the importance and nature of the translator's task. In the preface to his translation, *Le Premier Livre de la Metamorphose,* Marot proposes to

> mieulx faire entendre et sçavoir à
> ceulx qui n'ont la langue latine, de
> quelle sorte il [Ovid] escrivoit, et quelle
> différence peult estre entre les anciens
> et les modernes. Oultre plus, tel
> lit en maint passage les noms d'Apollo,
> Daphné, Pyramus et Tisbée, qui a
> l'histoire aussi loing de l'esprit
> que les noms près de la bouche; ce qui
> pas ainsi ne iroit si en facile vulgaire

---

(14) He was probably the first poet anywhere to use *canzone* 323. Bruce W. Wardropper, *Historia de la poesia lyrica a lo divino en la cristiandad occidental* (Madrid: Revista de Occidente, 1958), pp. 263-264, discusses an Italian work which inaugurated a tradition of Petrarch as a spiritual poet, the *Dialogo del dolce morire di Gesù Christo sopra le sei Visioni di M. Francesco Petrarca* (1544), written by Feliciano Umbruno da Civitella. In this case, the *canzone* is the subject of a theological conversation between the Signora Giacopa Pallavicina da Parma and a certain Leonzio.

(15) See P. M. Smith, *Clément Marot: Poet of the French Renaissance* (London: Athlone Press, 1970), pp. 55, 59, 77, 155, 249, 267-274.

(16) Mayer, «Clément Marot and Literary History,» p. 255.

(17) Sebillet, *Art Poétique françoys,* p. 116.

estoit mise cette belle Metamorphose,
laquelle aux poètes vulgaires et aux
painctres seroit trèsprouffitable, et
aussi decoration grande en nostre langue
... (18)

This reflects an already widely acceptable humanist practice,
spoken of by Thomas Sebillet in his *Art Poétique Françoys*
of 1548 and later by Du Bellay and Ronsard who set
forth the views of the next generation. Sebillet describes
translation as

aujourd'hui le Pöéme plus frequent et
mieus recue dés estimés Pöétes et dés
doctes lecteurs, a cause que chacun d'eus
estime grand oeuvre et de grand pris,
rendre la pure et argentine invention
dés Pöétes dorée et enrichie de notre
langue. Et vrayement celuy et son oeuvre
meritent grande louenge, qui a peu
proprement et naivement exprimer en
son langage, ce qu'un autre avoit mieus
escrit au sien, aprés l'avoir bien conceu
en son esperit. (19)

A comparison of *canzone* 323 and Marot's version brings to
light Marot's poetic abilities, the limitations of his poetic
idiom, and the appeal of «Standomi un giorno» to both the
translator and his audience. Marot's first problem was to find
a suitable equivalent for the *canzone* form, no great obstacle for

---

(18) Grenier, *Oeuvres complètes de Clément Marot*, II, 152.
(19) Sebillet, *Art Poétique françoys*, pp. 187-188. Sebillet's
treatise foreshadows much of what is to come in Du Bellay's
Deffence. In *Three Centuries of French Poetic Theory 1328-1630*
(Ann Arbor: Univ. of Michigan Press, 1935), I, 260, Warner Patterson
states that Sebillet's work is the first of the poetic treatises to
deal with the sonnet in France.

a poet experienced in the composition of a variety of longer lyrics. He turned to the *chant royal,* a verse form he had many times used for subjects of a serious nature, and entitled his translation «Le Chant des visions de Pétrarque.» A fairly fixed form, the *chant royal* consists of five stanzas of eleven lines each plus an envoy of five lines. Although no rhyme word is to appear twice, all the stanzas have the same five rhymes and end with a refrain (*ababccddede* for the stanzas and *ddede* for the envoy). The *canzone* is less fixed than the *chant royal,* but «Standomi un giorno» has the approximate length of a *chant royal.* Petrarch uses six stanzas of twelve lines, an envoy of three, and four basic rhymes throughout. Accommodating the *canzone* to the French language, Marot devises an orderly form of six stanzas with twelve lines each. He is forced, nonetheless, to use five different rhymes in each stanza, but the pattern is always *abaabbccdeed.*

Marot also uses a decasyllabic line rather than the combination of hendecasyllabic and seven-syllable lines in the original. The ten-syllable line, at that time, was the choice of poets who wrote on serious or heroic subjects, and was, therefore, fitting for the serious matter in Petrarch's poem. (20) At this stage in the development of the French language, the decasyllable is a long metrical unit and requires that Marot expand and add to the original. (21) At times his additions reflect

---

(20) See Joseph Vianey, «L'Art du vers chez Clément Marot» in *Mélanges Abel Lefranc* (Paris: Droz, 1936), pp. 44-57. Vianey discusses Marot's contributions to versification and his extensive use of the ten-syllable line, the line which Sebillet (*Art Poétique françoys,* pp. 39-40) saw as the heroic line *par excellence.*

(21) Charles Camproux, «Langue et métrique: à propos du decasyllabe des 'Epîtres' de Marot,» *FM,* 32 (1964), 194-205, discusses why the decasyllabic line was preferable for serious or heroic verse at the time of Marot as well as at the time of Ronsard who undertook to write his *Franciade* in verses of ten syllables. Camproux claims that this involves a linguistic problem, since the structure of the French language was undergoing some important changes during the sixteenth century. For a language that used particularly short words, such as the development of the language had created, the decasyllable offered a long meter. This same meter became

his understanding of the important elements of the poem and show his mettle as a translator. Paul Goodman comments that a good translation «is grounded in practical formal criticism ... [and that] the translator must estimate just what parts are strongly functioning in giving the effect.» (22)

Accordingly, in his adaptation of the visionary structure of «Standomi un giorno,» Marot enhances the basic fiction of the poem. By adding *devant mes yeulx,* Marot strengthens the illusion that the events have actually been seen:

> Un jour estant seulet à la fenestre,
> Vey tant de cas noveaulx devant mes yeulx,
> Que d'en tant veoir fasché me convint estre.
> (lines 1-3)

Naturally, the seven-syllable lines of the original are enlarged upon. Sometimes Marot carries over a phrase from the preceding lines; sometimes he develops what is only implicit or emphasizes what seems important. In the vision of the phoenix, there is the sententious «Ogni cosa al fin vola.» Marot puts his equivalent «Toute chose enfin passe» in relief by the addition of a rhetorical question: «Que diray plus? Toute chose enfin passe.» In a similar manner he lengthens the outburst of the spectator in the vision of the fountain. Petrarch's «ond'ancor doglia sento, / E sol de la memoria mi sgomento,» is lengthened to two full lines: «Dont le mien cueur grand regret encor a; / Et y pensant, du seul penser je souffre.» Marot replaces the more dignified *doglia* and *me-*

---

rather short for a language which increasingly used words created from Latin. For a linguistic stage marked by parataxis, the meter would seem long, while the same meter would appear shorter for a linguistic stage characterized by hypotaxis. Camproux demonstrates this thesis with a close analysis of the grammatical elements in Marot's *Epîtres,* where the decasyllabic line seems as long as the alexandrine in the seventeenth century.

(22) *The Structure of Literature* (Chicago: Univ. of Chicago Press, 1968), p. 227.

moria with *regret* and *penser,* but adds the rhetorical interest of the *annominatio* by using *penser* as a noun.

At the same time, Marot's emendations occasionally alter the intensity or the focus of the original. For instance, Petrarch's fountain is a *locus amoenus* peopled with nymphs and muses whose songs harmonize with the sound of the water:

> *Chiara* fontana, in quel medesmo bosco,
> Sorgea d'un sasso, et acque *fresche e dolci*
> Spargea, soavemente mormorando:
> Al bel seggio, *riposto, ombroso* et *fosco,*
> Né pastori appressavan né bifolci,
> Ma ninfe e muse, *a quel tenor cantando*:
>
> (lines 37-42)

Petrarch selects few but precise details to suggest the aristocratic beauty and harmony of the place and uses words that suggest to the ear the melodious sounds he hears, especially the sibilants throughout to suggest the sound of water. Most of the special effects are lost in the translation as Marot modifies the complex of detail:

> Au mesmes boys sourdoit d'un vif rocher
> Fontaine d'eau murmurant soefvement;
> De ce lieu frais *tant excellent et cher*
> N'osoient pasteurs ne *bouviers* approcher,
> Mais mainte Muse et Nymphe seulement,
> *Qui de leurs voix accordoient doulcement*
> *Au son de l'eau.*
>
> (lines 37-42)

The sensual quality and noble tone of Petrarch's description are diminished because Marot omits or replaces the vivid, concrete modifiers such as *chiara, fresche, riposto, ombroso,* and *fosco* with general expressions such as *tant excellent et cher,* which make less specific the beauty and value of the fountain and its surroundings. And the imitative harmony of the original is lost.

Marot's modifications often reflect the yet unsettled state of the French poetic idiom. Generally, Marot does not succeed with the long, effective periodic sentences. Nor does he achieve the variety and felicity of phrasing that stand out in every line of the original. Marot's poetic language is not the equal of Petrarch's. (23) Petrarch's is a noble, «public» style while Marot's is slightly more «familiar.» In the vision of the fountain, *seggio* and *bifolci* are noble words, replaced by *lieu* and *bouviers.* The noble euphemism *portarsene seco* is changed to the more terre-à-terre *devora,* which underscores the drama of the catastrophe but deprives the passage of its delicacy and equilibrium with the intrusion of a note of violence. In some instances, Marot is able to find a poetic equivalent for the Italian or even to heighten the effects of the original. In his sketch of the fountain, Marot adds a hint of awe and wonder to the surroundings by writing that the shepherds and cowherds *dare* not approach the area: «De ce lieu frais tant excellent et cher / N'osoient pasteurs *ne* bouviers approcher.» Further, Marot adopts Petrarch's vocabulary (i. e., *tempeste, delictz, nue,* and *nef*), and retains the six central images.

Certain alterations in the language of the poem effect a change in the thematic focus. The recasting of the chase in the first vision is an example. Inviting the comparison with a particular fair lady, Petrarch envisions a fair wild creature with *fronte umana*:

> Cacciata da duo veltri, un nero, un bianco;
> Che l'un e l'altro fianco

---

(23) Although Leonard Forster, *The Icy Fire: Five Studies in European Petrarchism* (Cambridge: Univ. Press, 1969), pp. 77-83, claims that Marot, like Chaucer, was not trying to forge a new poetic language because he had one which he and his public found entirely satisfactory, there is some indication that Marot was concerned with improving and embellishing the French language.

De la fera *gentil* mordean sí forte,
Che 'n poco tempo la menaro al passo
Ove *chiusa in un sasso*
Vinse molta bellezza acerba morte:
(lines 6-11)

The black and white greyhounds were traditional symbols of
night and day, of the passage of time. (24) Petrarch is being
specific, since «chiusa in un sasso» refers to Laura's entomb-
ment. Marot's *bische* is not characterized by a *fronte umana*
nor is it pictured finally as a lady entombed. «Belle pour plaire
au souverain des dieux,» the *bische* is pursued and mortally
wounded by the two dogs:

Chassée estoit de deux *chiens envieux,*
Un blanc, un noir, qui par *mortel effort*
La gente beste aux flans mordoient si fort,
Qu'au dernier pas en bref temps l'ont menée
Cheoir soubz un roc. Et là, la cruaulté
De mort vainquit une grande beauté,
(lines 6-11)

For *veltri* Marot uses the more humble term *chiens.* He
stresses the idea of time and mutability by describing the
the *chiens* as *envieux,* the adjective traditionally applied to
time. (25)

---

(24) See Carducci, *Le Rime,* p. 440, n. 6.
(25) The theme of «devouring» or «envious» time is common
long before Shakespeare's famous nineteenth sonnet («Devouring
time blunt thou the Lyons Pawes»). The source of the phrase is
probably the apostrophe to time in the last book of Ovid's
Metamorphoses: «Tempus edax rerum, tuque, *invidiosa* vetus-
tas, / omnia destruitis vitiataque dentibus aevi / paulatim lenta
consumitis omnia morte» (lines 234-236). This follows an impressive
discourse on mutability (lines 179-236) delivered by Pythagoras. I
cite from *Metamorphoses with an English Translation by Frank
Justus Miller,* eds. E. Capps, T. E. Page, and W. H. D. Rouse
(London: Heinemann, 1927).

Likewise, in his description of the ship, Marot omits two details in the original which accentuate the metaphorical relationship between the ship and Laura. Petrarch describes his ship as «carca di ricca merce onesta»; it founders on a reef in the midst of a sudden *tempesta orïental*. The adjective *orïental* is a probable reference to the eastern origin of the plague which swept through Western Europe and of which Laura was a victim. (26) Marot's version omits both *onesta* and *orïental*:

> La belle nef pour sa charge portoit
> Riches tresors; mais tempeste subite,
> En troublant l'air, ceste mer tant irrite,
> Que la nef heurte un roc caché soubz l'onde.
>
> (lines 18-21)

By selectively altering the detail in Petrarch's *canzone,* Marot has modified its meaning, and Petrarch's constrained and melancoly lament is generalized and transformed into the dramatic conflict between the hope of preserving beauty and the inevitable despair over the end of all earthly things.

Marot's «Visions de Pétrarque» is a part of that self-conscious, humanist movement to create a new and brilliant national literature in France. It reflects the stage of the French language as well as Marot's abilities and intentions. Marot makes a stylistic contribution, moving away from the lighter, more humble and private style of the court poet toward a broader, more noble public style, and the difference between this translation of Petrarch and his earlier Petrarchan borrowings is marked. In this earlier phase, there is a mixture of medieval tradition and Petrarchist inspiration. Marot uses themes and devices which fit in with what he had inherited

---

(26) Ezio Chiòrboli, ed. *Francesco Petrarca: Le 'Rime Sparse'* (Milan: Trevisini, 1924), p. 735, n. 19-20, suggests this would be understood in a specific way and cites the introduction of Boccaccio's *Decameron* as the source of *orïental.*

from his predecessors. (27)   At times, Petrarchan themes are given totally un-Petrarchan twists.   In his translations, on the other hand, Marot writes not of the lover's woes and raptures but of the serious concerns of the bereaved poet-lover forced to consider the problem of change and death.   Furthermore, Marot, in this later phase, succeeds in imitating the Petrarchan forms.   With his «Chant des visions de Pétrarque,» Marot accommodates the *canzone* in French during a period in which he is also experimenting with the sonnet. (28)

Because of its style and themes, Marot's «Visions» is a poem in which the two movements of Petrarch's influence converge. At least one of Marot's contemporaries saw some similarities between this *canzone* and the *Trionfi,* for he published the two poems in a single volume. Because of its allegorical and moralistic content, (29) the *Trionfi* had found a receptive audience in France as early as the second half of the fifteenth century when the first French translation was written by Jean Robertet. (30) By comparison with the French versions of the *Trionfi,* which tended to paraphrase the content

---

(27) See Marcel Françon, «Pétrarque et Clément Marot,» *Italica,* 40 (1963), 19-20.

(28) Mayer («Le premier sonnet français») refutes Marcel Françon, «Notes sur l'histoire du sonnet en France,» *Italica,* 29 (1952), 121-128, and «La Date d'un sonnet de St.-Gelais,» *BHR,* 15 (1953), 213-214. In another article, «Sur l'influence de Pétrarque en France aux XVᶜ et XVIᵉ siècles,» *Italica,* 19 (1942), 106, Françon observes that Marot's translation of «O passi sparsi» served as a model for Ronsard. He adds that both poets translated or imitated «Chi vuol veder.» Some of Mayer's contentions are again disputed by Françon in «L'Introduction du sonnet en France,» pp. 62-67.

(29) D. D. Carnicelli, «Bernard Illicino and the Renaissance Commentaries on Petrarch's *Trionfi,*» *RPh,* 23 (1969), 58, claims that the widespread enthusiasm for the *Trionfi* from the fourteenth century to the middle of the sixteenth century «can be explained in part by medieval and early Renaissance predilection for allegory and high seriousness in poetry, for the *Trionfi* are in fact a series of allegorical poems depicting six successive stages in man's life, from his initial bondage to the flesh ('The Triumph of Love') to his eventual redemption through Christ and the Virgin ('The Triumph of Eternity').»

(30) Simone, *Il Rinascimento francese,* p. 179.

of the original, Marot's translation of «Standomi un giorno» is an unusually sophisticated reproduction. Nonetheless, in 1538, the printer Denis Janot of Paris printed Marot's «Visions» along with a new translation of the *Trionfi* by a lawyer and historian from Provence, Jean Meynier, baron d'Oppède. (31) This edition was reprinted in 1545 and 1547. (32) This joining of the «Visions» with the already popular *Trionfi* suggests why Marot was probably attracted to the poem in the first place: for its graphic pictorial qualities, its stately procession of emblematic images and figures, its noble diction and solemn music, its variety and color, its dramatic reversals of fortune and state (also expressed by the current popular *De casibus* tradition), its serious and universal theme. Moreover, the «Visions» and the *Trionfi* were soon disjoined again, the *Trionfi* to die out in France or to evolve into other forms, the «Visions» to be renewed, at least for a brief moment, by several great writers.

---

(31) Meynier's work, «Les Triumphes Petrarque traduictes de Tuscane en Rhime françoyse par le Baron d'Opede, avec privilege du Roy,» is accompanied by Marot's translation of Petrarch's *canzone* under the title, «Des Visions de Petrarque,» as well as by a *rondeau* on a religious subject. This information is given by C. A. Mayer, *Bibliographie des oeuvres de Clément Marot* (Geneva: Droz, 1954), p. 81.

(32) Simone, *Il Rinascimento francese*, p. 215, n. 1. Marcel Françon, «Vasquin Philieul, Traducteur de Pétrarque,» *FS*, 4 (1950), 218, explains that Marot's visions as well as five of the six sonnets were to become part of the first complete translation in French verse of Petrarch's *Rime, Toutes les euvres vulgaires de Françoys Pétrarque contenans quatre livres de M. D. Laure d'Avignon ... mis en Françoys par Vasquin Philieul de Carpentras, Docteur es Droictz.* This appeared in Avignon in 1555.

Chapter IV

DU BELLAY'S *SONGE*: THE CALAMITY OF ROME

SONGE

I

C'estoit alors que le present des Dieux
    Plus doulcement s'écoule aux yeux de l'homme,
    Faisant noyer dedans l'oubly du somme
    Tout le soucy du jour laborieux,
Quand un Demon apparut à mes yeux
    Dessus le bord du grand fleuve de Rome,
    Qui m'appellant du nom dont je me nomme,
    Me commanda regarder vers les cieux:
Puis m'escria, Voy (dit-il) & contemple
    Tout ce qui est compris sous ce grand temple,
    Voy comme tout n'est rien que vanité.
Lors cognoissant la mondaine inconstance,
    Puis que Dieu seul au temps fait resistance,
    N'espere rien qu'en la divinité.

II

Sur la croppe d'un mont je vis une Fabrique
    De cent brasses de hault: cent columnes d'un rond
    Toutes de diamant ornoient le brave front:
    Et la façon de l'œuvre estoit à la Dorique,

La muraille n'estoit de marbre ny de brique,
 Mais d'un luisant crystal, qui du sommet au fond
 Elançoit mille rayz de son ventre profond
 Sur cent degrez dorez du plus fin or d'Afrique.
D'or estoit le lambriz, & le sommet encor
 Reluisoit escaillé de grandes lames d'or:
 Le pavé fut de jaspe, & d'esmeraulde fine.
O vanité du monde! un soudain tremblement
 Faisant crouler du mont la plus basse racine,
 Renversa ce beau lieu depuis le fondement.

III

Puis m'apparut une Poincte aguisee
 D'un diamant de dix piedz en carré,
 A sa hauteur justement mesuré,
 Tant qu'un archer pourroit prendre visee.
Sur ceste Poincte une urne fut posee
 De ce metal sur tous plus honnoré:
 Et reposoit en ce vase doré
 D'un grand Cæsar la cendre composee.
Aux quatre coings estoient couchez encor
 Pour pedestal quatre grands lyons d'or,
 Digne tumbeau d'une si digne cendre.
Las rien ne dure au monde que torment!
 Je vy du ciel la tempeste descendre,
 Et fouldroyer ce brave monument.

IV

Je vy hault eslevé columnes d'ivoire,
 Dont les bases estoient du plus riche metal,
 A chapiteaux d'albastre, & frizes de crystal,
 Le double front d'un arc dressé pour la memoire.
A chaque face estoit protraicte une victoire,
 Portant ælles au doz, avec habit Nymphal,
 Et hault assise y fut sur un char triomphal
 Des Empereurs Romains la plus antique gloire.

L'ouvrage ne monstroit un artifice humain,
  Mais sembloit estre fait de celle propre main
  Qui forge en aguisant la paternelle fouldre.
Las je ne veulx plus voir rien de beau sous les cieux,
  Puis qu'un œuvre si beau j'ay veu devant mes yeux,
  D'une soudaine cheute estre reduict en pouldre.

V

Et puis je vy l'Arbre Dodonien
  Sur sept costaux espandre son umbrage,
  Et les vainqueurs ornez de son fueillage
  Dessus le bord du fleuve Ausonien.
Là fut dressé maint trophee ancien,
  Mainte despouille, & maint beau tesmoignage
  De la grandeur de ce brave lignage
  Qui descendit du sang Dardanien.
J'estois ravy de voir chose si rare,
  Quand de paisans une troppe barbare
  Vint oultrager l'honneur de ces rameaux.
J'ouy le tronc gemir sous la congnee,
  Et vy depuis la souche desdaignee
  Se reverdir en deux arbres jumeaux.

VI

Une Louve je vy sous l'antre d'un rocher
  Allaictant deux bessons. Je vis à sa mamelle
  Mignardement joüer ceste couple jumelle,
  Et d'un col allongé la Louve les lecher.
Je la vy hors de là sa pasture chercher,
  Et courant par les champs, d'une fureur nouvelle
  Ensanglanter la dent & la patte cruelle
  Sur les menus troppeaux pour sa soif estancher.
Je vy mille veneurs descendre des montagnes,
  Qui bornent d'un costé les Lombardes campagnes,
  Et vy de cent espieux luy donner dans le flanc.

Je la vy de son long sur la plaine estendue
  Poussant mille sanglotz, se veautrer en son sang,
  Et dessus un vieux tronc la despouille pendue.

VII

Je vy l'Oyseau, qui le soleil contemple,
  D'un foible vol au ciel s'avanturer,
  Et peu à peu ses ælles asseurer,
  Suivant encor le maternel exemple.
Je le vy croistre, & d'un voler plus ample
  Des plus hauts monts la hauteur mesurer,
  Percer la nue, & ses ælles tirer
  Jusques au lieu, où des Dieux est le temple.
Là se perdit; puis soudain je l'ay veu
  Rouant par l'air en tourbillon de feu,
  Tout enflammé sur la plaine descendre.
Je vy son corps en poudre tout reduit,
  Et vy l'oyseau, qui la lumiere fuit,
  Comme un vermet renaistre de sa cendre.

VIII

Je vis un fier Torrent, dont les flots escumeux
  Rongeoient les fondemens d'une vieille ruine:
  Je le vy tout couvert d'une obscure bruine,
  Qui s'eslevoit par l'air en tourbillons fumeux:
Dont se formoit un corps à sept chefz merveilleux,
  Qui villes & chasteaux couvoit sous sa poittrine,
  Et sembloit devorer d'une egale rapine
  Les plux doulx animaux, & les plus orgueilleux.
J'estois esmerveillé de voir ce monstre enorme
  Changer en cent façons son effroyable forme,
  Lors que je vy sortir d'un antre Scythien
Ce vent impetueux, qui soufle la froidure,
  Dissiper ces nuaux, & en si peu que rien
  S'esvanouïr par l'air ceste horrible figure.

IX

Tout effroyé de ce monstre nocturne,
    Je vis un Corps hydeusement nerveux,
    A longue barbe, à long flottans cheveux,
    A front ridé, & face de Saturne:
Qui s'accoudant sur le ventre d'une urne,
    Versoit une eau, dont le cours fluctueux
    Alloit baignant tout ce bord sinueux,
    Où le Troyen combattit contre Turne.
Dessous ses piedz une Louve allaictoit
    Deux enfançons: sa main dextre portoit
    L'arbre de paix, l'autre la palme forte:
Son chef estoit couronné de laurier:
    A donc luy cheut la palme, & l'olivier,
    Et du laurier la branche devint morte.

X

Sur la rive d'un fleuve une Nymphe esploree
    Croisant les bras au ciel avec mille sanglotz
    Accordoit ceste plainte au murmure des flotz,
    Oultrageant son beau teinct, & sa tresse doree:
Las où est maintenant ceste face honoree,
    Où est ceste grandeur, & cet antique los,
    Où tout l'heur & l'honneur du monde fut enclos.
    Quand des hommes j'estois, & des Dieux adoree?
N'estoit-ce pas assez que le discord mutin
    M'eut fait de tout le monde un publique butin,
    Si cet Hydre nouveau digne de cent Hercules,
Foisonnant en sept chefz de vices monstrueux
    Ne m'engendroit encor à ces bords tortueux
    Tant de cruelz Nerons, & tant de Caligules?

XI

Dessus un mont une Flamme allumee
    A triple pointe ondoyoit vers les cieux,

Qui de l'encens d'un cedre precieux
Parfumoit l'air d'une odeur embasmee:
D'un blanc oyseau l'ælle bien emplumee
Sembloit voler jusqu'au sejour des Dieux,
Et dégoisant un chant melodieux
Montoit au ciel avecques la fumee:
De ce beau feu les rayons escartez,
Lançoient par tout mille & mille clartez,
Quand le degout d'une pluie doree
Le vint esteindre. O triste changement!
Ce qui sentoit si bon premierement,
Fut corrumpu d'une odeur sulphuree.

XII

Je vy sourdre d'un roc une vive Fonteine,
Claire comme crystal aux rayons du soleil,
Et jaunissant au fond d'un sablon tout pareil
A celuy que Pactol' roule parmy la plaine.
Là sembloit que nature & l'art eussent pris peine
D'assembler en un lieu tous les plaisirs de l'oeil:
Et là s'oyoit un bruit incitant au sommeil,
De cent accords plus doulx que ceulx d'une Sirene.
Les sieges & relaiz luisoient d'ivoire blanc,
Et cent Nymphes autour se tenoient flanc à flanc,
Quand des monts plus prochains de Faunes une suyte
En effroyables criz sur le lieu s'assembla,
Qui de ses villains piedz la belle onde troubla,
Mist les sieges par terre, & les Nymphes en fuyte.

XIII

Plus riche assez que ne se monstroit celle
Qui apparut au triste Florentin,
Jettant ma veüe au rivage Latin
Je vy de loing surgir une Nasselle:
Mais tout soudain la tempeste cruelle,
Portant envie à si riche butin,

Vint assaillir d'un Aquilon mutin
La belle Nef des autres la plus belle.
Finablement l'orage impetueux
Fit abysmer d'un gouphre tortueux
La grand' richesse à nulle autre seconde.
Je vy sous l'eau perdre le beau thresor,
La belle Nef, & les Nochers encor,
Puis vy la Nef se ressourdre sur l'onde.

XIV

Ayant tant de malheurs gemy profondement,
Je vis une Cité quasi semblable à celle
Que vit le messager de la bonne nouvelle,
Mais basty sur le sable estoit son fondement.
Il sembloit que son chef touchast au firmament,
Et sa forme n'estoit moins superbe que belle:
Digne, s'il en fut onc, digne d'estre immortelle,
Si rien dessous le ciel se fondoit fermement.
J'estois esmerveillé de voir si bel ouvrage,
Quand du costé du Nort vint le cruel orage,
Qui souflant la fureur de son coeur despité
Sur tout ce qui s'oppose encontre sa venüe,
Renversa sur le champ, d'une pouldreuse nüe,
Les foibles fondemens de la grande Cité.

XV

Finablement sur le poinct que Morphee
Plus veritable apparoit à noz yeux,
Fasché de voir l'inconstance des cieux,
Je voy venir la soeur du grand Typhee:
Qui bravement d'un morion coeffee
En majesté sembloit egale aux Dieux,
Et sur le bord d'un fleuve audacieux
De tout le monde erigeoit un trophee.
Cent Roys vaincuz gemissoient à ses piedz
Les bras aux doz honteusement liez:
Lors effroyé de voir telle merveille,

Le ciel encor je luy voy guerroyer,
    Puis tout à coup je la voy fouldroyer,
    Et du grand bruit en sursault je m'esveille. (1)

At a time when Marot's «Visions de Pétrarque» was still in circulation, Joachim Du Bellay, a poet of the next generation, made his own contribution to this growing family of visionary poems. He did not translate; he adapted «Standomi un giorno» and renewed it as a symbolic expression of the calamities which assailed ancient Rome and of its reduction to ruins. Du Bellay entitled his imitation *Songe* and appended it to his *Antiquitez de Rome,* published in 1558. *Songe* has not engendered much discussion among modern critics since Joseph Vianey dismissed the work as «trop artificielle pour qu'il y ait le moindre intérêret à rechercher où du Bellay en a emprunté les éléments.» (2) Even the latest book on Du Bellay tells us that *Songe* is «a hermetically sealed mystery» in which not only «the enigma but the fantasy tend to be regarded as a squandering of talent.» (3) These judgments assume much in the name of the reader and ignore both the popularity and the history of the poem in the Renaissance.

To begin with, *Songe* is an example of *imitatio,* that principle which justified the Renaissance poets' necessarily plagiaristic methods of enriching their languages and introducing new poetic forms into their national literatures. In his *Deffence,* Du Bellay himself draws a fine line between translation and imitation. The former he says is the reproduction of a text and the latter a process whereby the poem is never to be taken over into another language exactly as it

---

(1) All quotations from *Les Regrets, Les Antiquitez de Rome,* and *Songe* are taken from Joachim Du Bellay, *Les Regrets et autres oeuvres poëtiques,* eds. J. Joliffe and M. A. Screech (Geneva: Droz, 1956). Henceforth, only the poem and line numbers will be cited in the text.

(2) *Le Pétrarquisme en France,* p. 334.

(3) L. Clark Keating, *Joachim du Bellay* (New York: Twayne, 1971), pp. 95-96.

stands. The codifier of Pléiade poetics, therefore, recommends that the imitator «sonde diligemment son naturel, & se compose à l'immitation de celuy dont il se sentira approcher de plus pres. Autremeñt son immitation ressembleroit celle du singe.» (4) He defines proper literary borrowing in an often cited metaphor which pictures the Romans

> immitant les meilleurs aucteurs Grecz, se transformant en eux, les devorant, & apres les avoir bien digerez, les convertissant en sang & nouriture, se proposant, chacun selon son naturel & l'argument qu'il vouloit elire, le meilleur aucteur, dont ilz observoint diligemment toutes les plus rares & exquises vertuz, & icelles comme grephes ... entoint & apliquoint à leur langue. (5)

Emile Faguet calls this a process of *innutrition*. (6)

Songe exemplifies this theory of *imitatio* which allowed and encouraged the vogue of families of poems. A number of Du Bellay's images and techniques derive from Petrarch and Marot, (7) from Latin authors, the Bible, and Roman history, (8) and are blended together in a distinctly individual

---

(4) Joachim Du Bellay, *La Deffence et Illustration de la langue françoyse*, ed. Henri Chamard (Paris: Didier, 1948), pp. 106-107.

(5) *Ibid.*, pp. 42-43.

(6) Emile Faguet, *Seizième siècle: Études littéraires* (Paris: Boivin, n. d.), pp. 214-215.

(7) Although his remarks in the *Deffence* about Clément Marot tend to be derogatory, one may assume that Du Bellay knew and appreciated the poetry of his predecessor. In *Seizième siècle*, pp. 294-295, Faguet points out the contradictions between the theory of the *Deffence* and Du Bellay's actual practice, and that Du Bellay «n'est pas si dur qu'on pourrait le croire pour les poètes de l'École qui précède la sienne. Il a loué Saint-Gelais; il a chanté Marot, et en jolis vers.» Faguet quotes an epitaph Du Bellay wrote for Marot which he describes in a note (p. 295) as «un demi-pastiche, très respectueux et très aimable, de la manière de Marot.»

(8) The sources of Du Bellay's imagery have been thoroughly discussed by V.-L. Saulnier, «Commentaires sur les *Antiquitez de Rome*,» *BHR*, 12 (1950), 114-143; Frank M. Chambers, «Lucan and the *Antiquitez de Rome*,» *PMLA*, 60 (1945), 937-948; Alfred Adler,

manner. (9) The poet's dream occurs when the dreamer is asleep:

C'estoit alors que le present des Dieux
    Plus doulcement s'écoule aux yeux de l'homme,
    Faisant noyer dedans l'oubly du somme
    Tout le soucy du jour laborieux,
Quand un Demon apparut à mes yeux
    Dessus le bord du grand fleuve de Rome,
    Qui m'appellant du nom dont je me nomme,
    Me commanda regarder vers les cieux:

                            (*Songe* I, lines 1-8)

These lines recall the first words of Aeneas's account of his crucial vision of Hector, when Hector advised him to flee from burning Troy during the final defeat of the Trojans by the Greeks. (10) In this way, Du Bellay can allude to the fateful beginnings of the Roman empire, which is his subject, as well as to the fact that this is his personal vision of Rome's destruction brought to him especially by the *daimon,* who had brought the earlier epic story of Rome's beginnings to Virgil. As Hector in the *Aeneid* brings significant advice to Aeneas, so the *Demon* (the Greek *daimon*) brings to the sleeper a significant message. Yet, for this poet, the inevitability of the natural cycle of decay and destruction is difficult to accept. Through the spectacle of mutability and degeneration, the sensibilities of the sleeper are gradually aroused, and in the closing sonnet, he awakens with a start, as from a nightmare,

---

«Du Bellay's *Antiquitez* XXXI: Structure and Ideology,» *BHR*, 13 (1951), 191-195; and John C. Lapp, «Mythological Imagery in Du Bellay,» *SP*, 61 (1964), 109-127.

    (9) Saulnier, «Commentaires sur les *Antiquitez*,» p. 138, shows that the source of the title is not only Petrarch but includes St. John the Divine, Cicero, and Plato.

    (10) See *Virgil with an English Translation by H. Rushton Fairclough,* rev. ed. (Cambridge: Harvard Univ. Press, 1960), I, 312, lines 268-273.

«sur le poinct que Morphee / Plus veritable apparoit à noz yeux» (*Songe* XV, lines, 1-2). (11)

Du Bellay's *Songe* is a cycle of fifteen sonnets, each of which describes an apparition symbolic of Rome. The *Demon* and Morpheus provide a frame for the poem which M. A. Screech describes as «un seul poème dont les stances, nouvelle démonstration de la virtuosité de Du Bellay, ont forme de sonnets.» (12) Sonnets in decasyllabic lines alternate with sonnets in alexandrines. The poet regularly rhymes the octave of each sonnet *abbaabba,* varying the sestet between *ccdeed* and *ccdede.* Often he opposes the octave and sestet to emphasize the movement from peace and beauty to destruction or change; sometimes the rhyme is an organizational device, such as when the second portion of the vision is enclosed in the four lines rhymed *deed.* Kurt Reichenberger claims that in sonnets II, III, and IV, the perception of truth and the moment of total destruction comes in the final tercet. (13) In the sestet of the introductory sonnet, the poet achieves integration through his rhyme, his use of adverbs of time (*puis, lors*) and the repetition of the command *voy.*

As usual in this visionary mode, repetition is an important device. The poet follows Petrarch in reproducing the phantasmagoric effect of the events in a dream. A simple sequence of events in rapid succession is knit together by the adverb *puis* and, in this case, the almost excessive reiteration of the phrase «je vy.» Du Bellay too brings about that illusion of visual reality which even the most fanciful dreams possess, but he draws this dream to a conclusion in the final sonnet with a shift to the present tense for greater immediacy. John Lapp points out that the significant difference between *Songe*

(11) For a discussion of the symbolism involving Morpheus, the source of which is Ovid's *Metamorphoses,* see Saulnier, «Commentaires sur les *Antiquitez,*» p. 122.

(12) See M. A. Screech's introduction to *Les Regrets et autres oeuvres poëtiques,* p. 39.

(13) Kurt Reichenberger, «Das Italienerlebnis Du Bellays: Die Thematik des 'Songe', und seine Beziehung zur manieristischen Ideenwelt,» *ZfrPh,* 82 (1966), 263.

and *Les Antiquitez* lies in the use of time. He claims that unlike *Les Antiquitez* where «the spectacle of Rome evokes precise images out of the past, the visionary sonnets of *Songe* suppress time, suggesting through simultaneity the evil implicit in virtue, the flaw in majesty, the weakness in power.» (14) The simultaneity and suppression of time which Lapp sees in this poem are due to the dream structure, to the poet's effort to give his *Songe* the full impact of a dream. Also, the poet repeats words like *soudain* to create a sense of rapidity and to introduce the element of shock.

The structure of the poem seems to require that the poet forego certain rhetorical devices common elsewhere in his poetry. Du Bellay seeks a form different from that in *Les Regrets* or *Les Antiquitez*. There are no invocations or addresses to the spirits of ancient Rome, the «Divins Esprits»; no *jeux de mots* to match the play on the word Rome in «Nouveau venu qui cherches Rome en Rome»; no elaborate comparisons such as «Telle que dans son char la Berecynthienne» or similes such as «Comme le champ semé en verdure foisonne»; no anaphorically organized sonnets such as «Ny la fureur de la flamme enragee»; no catalogues of cultural treasures, as in «Tout ce qu'Egypte en poincte façonna.» Rather, the images are marshalled in the manner of Petrarch; the stylistic effects are subordinate to the visionary framework and content of the poem.

The poet's ingenuity shows itself mainly in the delineation of the central images. Drawn from a wide range of sources, the images in *Songe* are architectural, topographical, botanical, zoological, Biblical, mythological, and nautical, but are selected for their specific literary, historical, and mythological associations. *Songe,* like *canzone* 323, derives from a matter of concern to the poet; its imagery owes its distinctiveness not only to the subject of *Les Antiquitez de Rome,* but also to the imagination of the poet himself. Du Bellay describes not the

---

(14) Lapp, «Mythological Imagery in Du Bellay,» p. 126.

ruins of Rome in *Songe,* but the noble ancient edifices themselves and their destruction. Hence, there is little of the *sentiment des ruines,* but much of the pathos of sudden calamity that characterizes the earlier visions. (15)

Du Bellay deals with his central images in a variety of ways, although he subdues the rhetorical richness typical of *Les Antiquitez.* The first three sonnets in *Songe* are visions of imaginary man-made monuments, *une Fabrique, une Poincte,* and *un arc,* reminiscent of images in *Les Antiquitez* where the depiction of Rome's physical dimensions enhances the reader's apprehension of Rome's cultural, economic, political, and social greatness. An almost technical assessment of the architectural composition of the *Fabrique* includes some striking measurements:

> Sur la croppe d'un mont je vis une Fabrique
> De cent brasses de hault: cent columnes d'un rond
> Toutes de diamant ornoient le brave front:
> Et la façon de l'œuvre estoit à la Dorique.
> *(Songe* II, lines 1-4)

Likewise, the proportions of the «Poincte» are awesome:

> Puis m'apparut une Poincte aguisee
> D'un diamant de dix piedz en carré,
> A sa hauteur justement mesuré,
> Tant qu'un archer pourroit prender visee.
> *(Songe* III, lines 1-4)

That such details are not only intended to aid the reader's imagination is apparent because the remaining modifiers do

---

(15) Du Bellay was not the first to use the sonnet form for a subject other than love. In *Le Pétrarquisme en France,* p. 336, Vianey states that the *Cento sonetti di M. Alisandro Piccolomini* (1549) announced a new subject for sonnets—satire—and that the Italians suggested the idea of treating the *sentiment des ruines* in sonnet form.

little to create precise and individualized pictures. As in *Les Antiquitez* or «Standomi un giorno,» the details are always subordinate to the meaning. Du Bellay creates a world of fantasy as had Petrarch, and we seldom get a clear picture of the Rome he knew at firsthand. At the same time, these physical dimensions lend precision to the pictures, a desirable concreteness to the visionary poetry. They demand that we perceive the *grandeur* of monuments regarded as *beau, brave,* or *digne* and constructed of diamond, gold, crystal, marble, emerald, ivory, and alabaster. In these early sonnets, the ubiquitous image of gold is a mark of the magnificence and splendor of Roman civilization. This typical, decorous, significant diction works less to define the singular aspects of the image than to denote its aristocratic nature and its cultural value.

In other sonnets, Du Bellay uses a slightly different means of establishing the metaphorical meaning of his images. At times, he introduces some image of Rome's physical aspect, at others some traditional symbol of Roman culture. The ninth sonnet, for instance, exhibits an image symbolic of Roman topography. The dreamer remembers the sight of what seems to be a statue:

> Je vis un Corps hydeusement nerveux,
> A longue barbe, à long flottans cheveux,
> A front ridé, & face de Saturne:
> Qui s'accoudant sur le ventre d'une urne,
> Versoit une eau, dont le cours fluctueux
> Alloit baignant tout ce bord sinueux,
> Où le Troyen combattit contre Turne.
>
> (*Songe* IX, lines 2-8)

This godly figure is the mythological father Tiber whose urn is the riverhead, the source of water, a giver and taker of life. Amplifying his image, Du Bellay again alludes to the *Aeneid,* which comes to a close with Aeneas' victory over Turnus on the bank of the Tiber, a defeat which marks the beginning of Rome's dominance in the world and the passing of the indigenous pastoral society. However, this latter decline also prefigures the inevitable fall of Rome and implies the cyclical nature of earthly existence in which birth is also the initiator of decay. Secondary imagery from Roman mythology extends and further defines the central metaphor:

> Dessous ses piedz une Louve allaictoit
>   Deux enfançons: sa main dextre portoit
>   L'arbre de paix, l'autre la palme forte:
> Son chef estoit couronné de laurier:
>   A donc luy cheut la palme, & l'olivier,
>   Et du laurier la branche devint morte.
>   (*Songe* IX, lines 9-12)

In the final lines, the poet alludes to the rise and fall of Roman civilization. The symbols of the founding of Rome, of the peace, victory, and poetic excellence she brought to the world, are incorporated into the image of the river god to create a metaphor of the birth and death of Roman culture.

In sonnets V, VI, and VII, biological metaphors for Rome derive from myth: the dreamer sees «l'Arbre Dodonien,» «Une Louve,» and «l'Oyseau qui le soleil contemple.» The seventh sonnet differs, because the poet combines three avian legends, those of the eagle, the phoenix, and the owl, in what Margaret Brady Wells calls a hierarchy of birds. (16) The eagle is a metaphor of Rome destroyed at the height of her power, the phoenix of Rome's rebirth, and the owl of Rome's lesser modern state, the corruption of which the poet feels so sharply. Jupiter's eagle was a kingly, high-flying bird which could soar in the face of the sun (17):

> Je vy l'Oyseau, qui le soleil contemple,
>   D'un foible vol au ciel s'avanturer,

---

(16) Margaret Brady Wells, «Du Bellay's Sonnet Sequence, *Songe*,» *FS*, 26 (1972), 5.

(17) Saulnier, «Commentaires sur les *Antiquitez*,» attempts to

Et peu à peu ses ælles asseurer,
Suivant encor le maternel exemple.
Je le vy croistre, & d'un voler plus ample
Des plus hauts monts la hauteur mesurer,
Percer la nue, & ses aelles tirer
Jusques au lieu, où des Dieux est le temple.

(*Songe* VII, lines 1-8)

The eagle's maturation and the development of his daring parallels the Titan motif in *Les Antiquitez* where the seven hills of Rome are seen as a threat to the power and majesty of the gods. (18) Roman pride is compared to that of the Titans, who were bound to fall:

Telz que lon vid jadis les enfans de la Terre
... ...
Tel encor' on a veu par dessus les humains
Le front audacieux des sept costaux Romains
Lever contre le ciel son orgueilleuse face:

(*Les Antiquitez* 12, lines 1, 9-11)

In John Lapp's opinion, all the elements of the central myth of the giants central to *Les Antiquitez* may be found in the *Songe,* which, the poet tells us on the title page, concerns «le mesme subject,» with its references to the seven hills whose very form constitutes an act of defiance, to the battle against Heaven, and to the final cataclysm and burial. (19)

In the sonnet of the eagle, the tragic cycle of *hubris* and

---

classify the images in *Songe*. He mentions Bruno Latini's description of the eagle in his *Tresor* as a source for this image. Du Bellay uses the same description of the eagle in another poem, «Les Tragiques Regrets de Charles V Empereur.»

(18) Such imagery is important in *Les Antiquitez* where Du Bellay mentions the seven hills of Rome in sonnets 2, 7, and 12. He also mentions them in the fifth sonnet of *Songe*.

(19) Lapp, «Mythological Imagery in Du Bellay,» p. 126.

nemesis is emphasized by the opposition of the octave and sestet; elsewhere this cycle provides one sort of unity to *Songe*. The intimation that the arch could be the work of Vulcan causes the reader to perceive its supreme excellence and the audacity of its creators:

> L'ouvrage ne monstroit un artifice humain,
>   Mais sembloit estre fait de celle propre main
>   Qui forge en aguisant la paternelle fouldre.
>   (*Songe* IV, lines 9-11)

In spite of its architectural superiority and beauty, the arch is mysteriously «reduict en poudre.» Possibly we should see this as the *nemesis* of an Arachne-like challenge to the artistry of a god. Finally, at the termination of *Songe,* an allusion to the myth of the giants appears once again when the sister of Typhoeus, a hero sometimes confused with the Titans, is struck by a thunderbolt, as are all those who challenge the gods. The dreamer sees the «soeur du grand Typhee» who

> En majesté sembloit egale aux Dieux,
>   Et sur le bord d'un fleuve audacieux
>   De tout le monde erigeoit un trophee.
>   (*Songe* XV, lines 6-8)

The mythological Typhoeus the last and most horrible of Earth's children to challenge Zeus after his defeat of the Titans, had no sister, according to Saulnier, and we must, therefore, understand the reference metaphorically: «la guerrière qui paraît ici pour symboliser Rome, c'est Rome elle-même qui est de la race des Typhées, digne de Typhée et à lui comparable.» (20) To clarify his meaning, Du Bellay creates a mythological

---

(20) Saulnier, «Commentaires sur les *Antiquitez*,» p. 123, goes on to explain that Typhoeus was a hero with one hundred heads (*Aeneid* VIII, lines 289-299), and like Rome produced numerous infants. After his defeat, he was buried by Etna or another mountain, like Rome under her seven hills. The heroic adventure

figure worthy both of Rome and of the wrath and punishment of Jupiter himself.

The fall of Rome was not wrought by the anger of the gods or by natural law alone. Toward the beginning of *Songe,* the dreamer seems primarily preoccupied with the question of natural destruction and decay. In the third sonnet, this dreamer follows in the tradition of Petrarch's *persona* who infers from his experience, «Ahi nulla altro che pianto al mondo dura!» Du Bellay's words follow exactly the line in Marot's translation with one notable exception. Marot's «Las! rien ne dure au monde que tristesse» is transposed into a new key with the substitution of *torment* for *tristesse.* Du Bellay's poem does not, however, rest on this simply pessimistic note.

Du Bellay tries to reveal something of the complexity of the natural processes while taking into account the human element. In the tenth sonnet, we see a nymph, the imaginative embodiment of the Roman Republic which had fallen victim to «*civile fureur.*» The development of the image in this poem is an exception to the poetic norm; we no longer have an unthinking thing or creature viewed by the sleeper but another supernatural guide. The prophetic tone of the *Demon,* with his allusion to Ecclesiastes and the preacher's admonition that all is vanity, is reinforced by the two long rhetorical questions posed by the nymph. She first asks:

> Las où est maintenant ceste face honoree,
> Où est ceste grandeur, & cet antique los,
> Où tout l'heur & l'honneur du monde fut enclos,
> Quand des hommes j'estois, & des Dieux adoree?
> (*Songe* X, lines 5-8)

The *ubi sunt* device (also found in *Les Antiquitez*), which is the stylistic analogue of the *vanitas vanitatum* theme, emphasizes the essential incomprehensibility of mutability with

---

of Typhoeus is similar to that of the giants and like Rome, Typhoeus is, in fact, the successor to the giants (see Virgil, *Georgics* I, lines 278 ff.).

its anaphorical repetition of *où*. If all things are subject to change, even the most magnificent works of man and nature are vainglories, and God remains man's only hope.

The catastrophe which has befallen the Roman Republic does not stop with the loss of honor, grandeur, law, or happiness. The second rhetorical question reveals that the Romans also underwent a process of moral degeneration:

> N'estoit-ce pas assez que le discord mutin
> M'eut fait de tout le monde un publique butin,
> Si cet Hydre nouveau digne de cent Hercules,
> Foisonnant en sept chefz de vices monstrueux
> Ne m'engendroit encor à ces bords tortueux
> Tant de cruelz Nerons, & tant de Caligules?
> (*Songe* X, lines 9-14)

Worse than immediate destruction was the slow death of the ideals of the Roman Republic. The catastrophe is, therefore, not a sudden unexpected blow but a gradual political, cultural, and moral deterioration associated with the reigns of the most cruel and degenerate emperors like Nero and Caligula.

In Petrarch's *canzone* the catastrophe is sudden and final. In *Songe* the situation is more complex. Some of the catastrophes in *Songe* follow Petrarch's example of immediate and irrevocable destruction—the palace, the obelisk, the arch, and the city with their nostalgia for Roman grandeur all come to a definitive end, it seems. Yet, in the dusty remains of the city, an image which lies in the penultimate position, we find also the hope of the New Jerusalem, the hope of rebirth. (21) Margaret Wells affirms the idea that ashes and dust may be a source of life and rebirth in both *Les Antiquitez* and *Songe*. Further, she argues that the underlying unity of *Songe* results from Du Bellay's extensive repetition of secondary elemental images of which only two or three occur in the Italian source.

---

(21) Wells, «Du Bellay's Sonnet Sequence,» p. 6.

The poet repeats particularly the images of fire and water, which are related to the natural cycle of birth and death. (22)

The catastrophes in *Songe* are sometimes similar to metamorphoses with their allusions to the rebirth and renewal implicit in creation. The eagle turns into an owl; the «Arbre Dodonien» is cut down, but the dreamer sees the trunk «se reverdir en deux arbres jumeaux.» The two sonnets directly inspired by images in «Standomi un giorno» show the essential difference in vision of the two poets. The fountain and the ship of «Standomi un giorno» are victims of natural disasters and are completely destroyed; their counterparts in *Songe* undergo drastic alterations, although their total destruction is never achieved. The «vive Fonteine» echoes Marot's use of the adjective *vif* and suggests the birth and grandeur of Rome, since water springing from a rock is a symbol of life. (23) Not a natural *locus amoenus,* Du Bellay's fountain is a sophisticated creation of artistically beautiful sights and sounds: (24)

> Là sembloit que nature & l'art eussent pris peine
> D'assembler en un lieu tous les plaisirs de l'oeil:
> Et là s'oyoit un bruit incitant au sommeil,
> De cent accords plus doulx que ceulx d'une Sirene.
>
> (*Songe* XII, lines 5-8)

Such a fountain belongs not to the pastoral atmosphere of the *Rime* but to the cultivated beauty of Rome described in *Les*

---

(22) *Ibid.,* pp. 1-8. Also, Guido Saba, *La poesia di Joachim du Bellay* (Florence: D'Anna, 1962), p. 139, speaks of the cyclical movement «per cui tutto nell'universo nasce, cresce, matura e muore.»

(23) Wells, *ibid.,* p. 3.

(24) In his book *Coronation of the Poet: Joachim du Bellay's Debt to the Trivium,* Univ. of California Publications in Modern Philology, No. 96 (Berkeley: Univ. of California Press, 1969), p. 124, Robert Griffin points out that Du Bellay may have been more influenced by Petrarch's «Chi vuol veder,» which he claims is the model for *Songe* XII. Du Bellay's description of the fountain, «Là sembloit que nature & l'art eussent pris peine,» echoes the idea of «Chi vuol veder,» but this sonnet can hardly be called an imitation of Petrarch's sonnet 248 as can sonnet 5 of *Les Antiquitez.*

Antiquitez as «tout ce qu'ont peu nature, / L'art, & le ciel» (*Les Antiquitez* 5, lines 1-2).

A comparison between the fountain in *Songe* and the beauty of ancient Rome is implicit in the classical allusions as well as in the catastrophe. The sounds of the fountain are not enchanting as they were in Petrarch. They are here the deranging sounds of the Sirens, which provide a suitable background for the shrieks of the fauns who bring havoc to this harmonious spot:

> Les sieges & relaiz luisoient d'ivoire blanc,
>> Et cent Nymphes autour se tenoient flanc à flanc,
>> Quand les monts plus prochains de Faunes une suyte
> En effroyables criz sur le lieu s'assembla,
>> Qui de ses villains piedz la belle onde troubla,
>> Mist les sieges par terre, & les Nymphes en fuyte.
>> (*Songe* XII, lines 9-14)

Clearly this is a catastrophe only in a figurative sense, since the fountain is not destroyed but left standing, a metaphor of Rome, sacked by the barbarians. The golden sands of the river Pactolus play a role in the fountain's ruin by attracting the envy of the Fauns, as the gold in the palace and obelisk had aroused the envy of the forces which wrought their destruction. The fauns symbolize those unpredictable forces in our world which may work changes either minor or radical in any created thing as well as those human appetites which may lead to degeneracy or *nemesis*. Here the two causes of Rome's downfall are subsumed in one image. The fauns are the actors in the poetic drama which forcefully illustrates Du Bellay's contention that the two earthly realms of creation, nature (God's creation) and art (man's creation) are part of the inevitable, on-going process that is life.

Du Bellay's *Songe* is imbued with a moral seriousness that goes beyond its expression of *Weltschmerz* or its warning against *hubris*. It has a complexity of tone that separates it from the pathos of Petrarch or from the grief of Marot. The intrusion of other than natural elements in these catastrophes creates an atmosphere which sets them off from «Standomi un giorno» or the «Visions de Pétrarque.» The sulfuric odor of Sonnet XI is «corrompu» and reminiscent of magic rituals or even hellfire; the sounds that intrude on the silence of this dream are disturbing. Kurt Reichenberger points out that the eerie silence of *Songe* is broken only by sounds which do not bring any relief, the sounds of the ax, the lament of the nymph, the death rattle of the she wolf, and the frightful cries of the fauns. (25) Such dissonance, the occasionally grotesque imagery, and the fear aroused by these sights call forth a partially different picture of Rome than the evenly tempered sonnets of *Les Antiquitez.*

The «torment» felt by the dreamer and the nightmarish cast of this dream cause Reichenberger to view this poem as an expression of European mannerism which demonized the harmonious elements of Renaissance art. He claims that the ghostly infernal atmosphere in *Songe* is typical of the mood of crisis which motivated so many manneristic visions of destruction. (26) The preoccupation with destruction is present in *Songe,* but Reichenberger exaggerates the nightmarish or manneristic qualities of the poem. In fact, *Songe* is not truly apocalyptic, and Du Bellay is always concerned with the spectacle of Rome's decline and the course of history rather than with human salvation, his or ours. The image of the new Jerusalem (Sonnet XIV) may well refer to the new Rome, the post-Constantine Papal Rome, which he had before his eyes in its fallen and shameful state. The images of beauty and proportion outweigh those of fear and destruction. The

---

(25) Reichenberger, «Das Italienerlebnis Du Bellays,» p. 264.

(26) *Ibid.,* pp. 265-266, compares the scenes of *Songe* with such manneristic manifestations as Raphael's frescoes in the Vatican, Michelangelo's Last Judgment and his vision of hell, Giulio Romano's battle of the Giants in the Palazzo del Té in Mantua, and a painting by Desiderio Monsù in which people are crushed by falling facades and vaults. On the other hand, Frédéric Boyer, *Joachim du Bellay* (Paris: Seghers, 1958), p. 86, comments: «Ces architectures incroyables, faites d'ivoire, d'or ou de diamants, aux

basic harmony, stateliness, and order of *Songe* derive from the artistic composition of the edifices and from the allusions to the natural cycle which limits the existence of all things.

Through his imaginary transformations of the mythological and historical past, Du Bellay recreates the history of Rome in his own way. As Petrarch's metaphors in «Standomi un giorno» were a shorthand for describing Laura and her death, the meaning generalized in Marot's translation, so the images in *Songe* are a means of poeticizing the disasters of Rome. The sonnets of *Songe* figure forth the decay and fall of Rome which serves as a symbol of the ineluctable power of the natural cycle. «Standomi un giorno» is a study in the psychology of love; *Songe* is an assessment of the nature of Rome's fall.

Songe is a «conversion ... en sang & nouriture» of the Italian *canzone,* and it reflects the stately seriousness of *Les Antiquitez,* with its praise of the ancient city. *Songe* is also a reaction to the latter. In this short sonnet cycle, Du Bellay assumes the stance of the cultural historian who appreciates Roman civilization, but who also understands that history records the rise and fall of civilizations. Time and change respect neither greatness nor beauty, and the monuments and symbols of the greatest civilization known to the Renaissance are prey to time like all creation. The pessimistic echo of Ecclesiastes, the warning that «tout n'est rien que vanité» (*Songe* I, line 11), leads Terrence Cave to view *Songe* as the precursor of the sermon type of poem. (27) Du Bellay alludes

---

proportions démesurées, et aux formes complexes, on en retrouve l'équivalent plastique dans les tableaux d'Antoine Caron. Ce baroquisme est un exemple curieux de ce qu'on pourrait appeler le délire humaniste, qui saisit parfois (trop rarement hélas) l'artiste de la Renaissance. On comprend alors que le concept d'Antiquité n'avait pas, à l'époque, la froideur raisonnable qu'il prendra chez les Classiques. Il est au contraire appréhendé par un esprit enthousiaste et violent, qui transforme son savoir en poésie, l'ordre intellectuel en désordre imaginatif et sentimental.»

(27) *Devotional Poetry in France, c. 1570-1613* (Cambridge: Cambridge Univ. Press, 1969), pp. 148-149.

to the Biblical *vanitas vanitatum* in the first sonnet, yet he never again returns to it. With such allusions, he is merely trying, as historians will, to appear wise and philosophical. Further, like most Renaissance poets, he acknowledges the Horatian *utile* by adding this wise and edifying maxim that everyone would recognize. This is not really devotional poetry, although it may have been useful to devotional poets.

As always, Du Bellay is singing «L'antique honneur du peuple à longue robbe» (*Les Antiquitez* 32, line 14), and what befell it; he is trying to be interesting and also pleasing, the Horatian *dulce*. All this visionary poetry with its striking pictorial images appeals to the eye and to the intellect. Its elaboration of the pathos of beauty, grandeur, and fame that fade responded to the Renaissance man's fascination with the melancholy instability of things. Thus, Du Bellay was attracted to Petrarch as was Marot, and he used the visionary device as a means of treating his favorite theme, Rome. Although this way of writing was soon to pass out of fashion, Du Bellay, like Marot, could still depend upon the popularity of the triumph-like review, the allegorical tableaux, the emblem, the dream-vision, the *De casibus* tradition, as well as the abiding interest in ancient Rome.

Chapter V

SPENSER'S MEDITATIONS ON THE WORLD'S VANITY

Visions of the Worlds Vanitie

1

One day, while that my daylie cares did sleepe,
My spirit, shaking off her earthly prison,
Began to enter into meditation deepe
Of things exceeding reach of common reason;
  Such as this age, in which all good is geason,
And all that humble is and meane debaced,
Hath brought forth in her last declining season,
Griefe of good mindes, to see goodnesse disgraced.
  On which when as my thought was throghly placed,
Vnto my eyes strange showes presented were,
Picturing that, which I in minde embraced,
That yet those sights empassion me full nere.
    Such as they were (faire Ladie) take in worth,
    That when time serues, may bring things better forth.

2

  In Summers day, when *Phœbus* fairly shone,
I saw a Bull as white as driuen snowe,
With gilden hornes embowed like the Moone,
In a fresh flowring meadow lying lowe:

Vp to his eares the verdant grasse did growe,
And the gay floures did offer to be eaten:
But he with fatnes so did ouerflowe,
That he all wallowed in the weedes downe beaten,
 Ne car'd with them his daintie lips to sweeten:
Till that a Brize, a scorned little creature,
Through his faire hide his angrie sting did threaten,
And vext so sore, that all his goodly feature,
 And all his plenteous pasture nought him pleased:
 So by the small the great is oft diseased.

3

Beside the fruitfull shore of muddie *Nile,*
Vpon a sunnie banke outstretched lay
In monstrous length, a mightie Crocodile,
That cram'd with guiltles blood, and greedie pray
 Of wretched people trauailing that way,
Thought all things lesse than his disdainfull pride.
I saw a little Bird, cal'd *Tedula,*
The least of thousands which on earth abide,
 That forst this hideous beast to open wide
The greisly gates of his deuouring hell,
And let him feede, as Nature doth prouide,
Vpon his iawes, that with blacke venime swell.
 Why then should greatest things the least disdaine,
 Sith that so small so mightie can constraine?

4

The kingly Bird, that beares *Ioues* thunder-clap,
One day did scorne the simple Scarabee,
Proud of his highest seruice, and good hap,
That made all other Foules his thralls to bee;
 The silly Flie, that no redresse did see,
Spide where the Eagle built his towring nest,
And kindling fire within the hollow tree,
Burnt vp his yong ones, and himselfe distrest;

Ne suffred him in anie place to rest,
But droue in *Ioues* own lap his egs to lay;
Where gathering also filth him to infest,
Forst with the filth his egs to fling away:
>   For which when as the Foule was wroth, said *Ioue,*
>   Lo how the least the greatest may reproue.

5

Toward the sea turning my troubled eye,
I saw the fish (if fish I may it cleepe)
That makes the sea before his face to flye,
And with his flaggie finnes doth seeme to sweepe
>   The fomie waues out of the dreadfull deep,
The huge *Leuiathan,* dame Natures wonder,
Making his sport, that manie makes to weep:
A sword-fish small him from the rest did sunder,
>   That in his throat him pricking softly vnder,
His wide Abysse him forced forth to spewe,
That all the sea did roare like heauens thunder,
And all the waues stain'd with filthie hewe.
>   Hereby I learned haue, not to despise
>   What euer thing seemes small in common eyes.

6

An hideous Dragon, dreadfull to behold,
Whose backe was arm'd against the dint of speare,
With shields of brasse, that shone like burnisht golde,
An forkhed sting, that death in it did beare,
>   Stroue with a Spider his vnequall peare:
And bad defiance to his enemie.
The subtill vermin creeping closely neare,
Did in his drinke shed poyson priuilie;
>   Which through his entrailes spredding diuersly,
Made him to swell, that nigh his bowells brust
And him enforst to yeeld the victorie,

That did so much in his owne greatnesse trust.
    O how great vainesse is it then to scorne
    The weake, that hath the strong so oft forlorne.

7

High on a hill a goodly Cedar grewe,
Of wondrous length, and streight proportion,
That farre abroad her daintie odours threwe;
Mongst all the daughters of proud *Libanon,*
    Her match in beautie was not anie one.
Shortly within her inmost pith there bred
A litle wicked worme, perceiu'd of none,
That on her sap and vitall moysture fed:
    Thenceforth her garland so much honoured
Began to die, (O great ruth for the same)
And her faire lockes fell from her loftie head,
That shortly balde, and bared she became.
    I, which this sight beheld, was much dismayed,
    To see so goodly thing so soone decayed.

8

Soone after this I saw an Elephant,
Adorn'd with bells and bosses gorgeouslie,
That on his backe did beare (as batteilant)
A gilden towre, which shone exceedinglie;
    That he himselfe through foolish vanitie,
Both for his rich attire, and goodly forme,
Was puffed vp with passing surquedrie,
And shortly gan all other beasts to scorne.
    Till that a little Ant, a silly worme,
Into his nosthrils creeping, so him pained,
That casting downe his towre, he did deforme
Both borrowed pride, and natiue beautie stained.
    Let therefore nought that great is, therein glorie,
    Sith so small thing his happines may varie.

9

Looking far foorth into the Ocean wide,
A goodly ship with banners brauely dight,
And flag in her top-gallant I espide,
Through the maine sea making her merry flight:
    Faire blew the winde into her bosome right;
And th'heauens looked louely all the while,
That she did seeme to daunce, as in delight,
And at her owne felicitie did smile.
    All sodainely there cloue vnto her keele
A little fish, that men call *Remora,*
Which stopt her course, and held her by the heele,
That winde nor tide could moue her thence away.
    Straunge thing me seemeth, that so small a thing
    Should able be so great an one to wring.

10

A mighty Lyon, Lord of all the wood,
Hauing his hunger throughly satisfide,
With pray of beasts, and spoyle of liuing blood,
Safe in his dreadles den him thought to hide:
    His sternesse was his prayse, his strength his pride,
And all his glory in his cruell clawes.
I saw a wasp, that fiercely him defide,
And bad him battaile euen to his iawes;
    Sore he him stong, that it the blood forth drawes,
And his proude heart is fild with fretting ire:
In vaine he threats his teeth, his tayle, his pawes,
And from his bloodie eyes doth sparkle fire;
    That dead himselfe he wisheth for despight.
    So weakest may anoy the most of might.

11

What time the Romaine Empire bore the raine
Of all the world, and florisht most in might,

The nations gan their soueraigntie disdaine,
And cast to quitt them from their bondage quight:
  So when all shrouded were in silent night,
The *Galles* were, by corrupting of a mayde,
Possest nigh of the Capitol through slight,
Had not a Goose the treachery bewrayde.
  If then a Goose great *Rome* from ruine stayde,
And *Ioue* himselfe, the patron of the place,
Preserud from being to his foes betrayde,
Why do vaine men mean things so much deface,
    And in their might repose their most assurance,
    Sith nought on earth can chalenge long endurance?

12

  When these sad sights were ouerpast and gone,
My spright was greatly moued in her rest,
With inward ruth and deare affection,
To see so great things by so small distrest:
  Thenceforth I gan in my engrieued brest
To scorne all difference of great and small,
Sith that the greatest often are opprest,
And vnawares doe into daunger fall.
  And ye, that read these ruines tragicall
Learne by their losse to love the low degree,
And if that fortune chaunce you vp to call
To honours seat, forget not what you be:
    For he that of himselfe is most secure,
    Shall finde his state most fickle and vnsure. (1)

FINIS

(1) The quotations from Spenser here and throughout are taken
from *The Works of Edmund Spenser: A Variorum Edition*, eds.
Edwin Greenlaw, *et al.* (Baltimore: Johns Hopkins Univ. Press,
1947), VIII, 174-178.

The history of Petrarch's popularity in England parallels that of his impact in France. First popular as a moral philosopher and an epic poet, he comes to be the poet moralist who creates a poetic language of love, who initiates humanistic studies in Europe, (2) and who is haunted by the sense that life is fleeting. Robert Coogan points out that by the mid-sixteenth century, the popularity of the *Trionfi* had brought together the notion of Petrarch the moralist with the notion of Petrarch as the lover of Laura. (3) The arrival of the visionary poetry in England coincides with this latter phase and also precedes the growth of the cult of amorous Petrarchism by approximately twenty years. These visionary poems may be considered the culmination of the movement initiated by the *Trionfi*. The visions of Petrarch, Marot, and Du Bellay were transported to England by the Dutch poet and moralist Jan van der Noot and were by him introduced to Edmund Spenser, the last of the significant contributors to this family of poems. (4).

---

(2) In *A Dialogue between Reason and Adversity: A Late Middle English Version of Petrarch's «De Remediis»* (Assen: Van Gorcum, 1968), pp. 25-32, F. N. M. Diekstra reveals that some dialogues of the *De Remediis* were put into English in the first quarter of the fifteenth century. He compares this with Petrarch's early reception on the continent, where, in the Netherlands, for example, Petrarch's reputation as a moralistic writer dated from a reference to the *De Remediis* in a treatise entitled *Somnium Doctrinale* (c. 1400) by Arnoldus Roterodamus (van Geilhoven), a monk interested in the moral writings of humanists.

(3) See his previously cited article, «Petrarch's *Trionfi* and the English Renaissance,» pp. 306-327, especially pp. 307, 315. See also Ivy L. Mumford, «Petrarchism in Early Tudor England,» *IS*, 19 (1964), 56-63, and D. G. Rees, «Petrarch's 'Trionfo della Morte' in English,» *IS*, 7 (1952), 82-96.

(4) There remains the possibility that Marot's translation of Petrarch's «Standomi un giorno» was available somewhat earlier in England. In the epistle to his translation of the *Trionfi*, Lord Morley relates that he had seen a French translation of the poems made for Francis I who rewarded the translator with one hundred crowns. Morley asserts that Francis took the book everyhere with him. See *Lord Morley's «Tryumphes of Fraunces Petrarcke»: The First English Translation of the «Trionfi»,* ed. D. D. Carnicelli

Forced from his home and family by the Spanish authorities because of his Protestant views, van der Noot engaged in compiling an emblem book which strongly denounces the Roman Church. (5) Interpreting the open-ended visionary metaphors in a religious manner, he found them entirely compatible with his personal protest. Entitled *Het Theatre,* the first edition of his little book appeared in London in 1568 and was composed entirely in Dutch. Van der Noot had translated Petrarch's *canzone* and eleven sonnets of Du Bellay's *Songe* into Dutch, to which he added four sonnets of his own composition, inspired by the book of Revelation. A series of woodcuts illustrated the poems and a commentary of considerable length explained the visions, expressing a strongly anti-Catholic feeling. The pictorial quality of this vision poetry and its historical association with moralistic writing made it suitable to an emblem book.

Wishing to reach the largest possible audience, van der Noot, still in London, published a French edition seven months later in 1568, an English edition in 1569, and a German edition in 1572. (6) In the French *Théâtre,* we find Marot's version of Petrarch divided into six epigrams, eleven of the sonnets from Du Bellay's *Songe,* plus the original four sonnets and the

---

(Cambridge: Harvard Univ. Press, 1971), pp. 77-78. In *Forty-Six Lives Translated from Boccaccio's «De Claris Mulieribus»* (London: Oxford Univ. Press, 1943), Herbert G. Wright, the editor, identifies the French translator spoken of by Lord Morley as the Baron d'Opède, whose version of the *Trionfi* had been published in Paris three times after 1538, with Marot's «Visions de Pétrarque.»

(5) In «Un Poète errant de la Renaissance: Jean van der Noot et l'Angleterre,» *RLC,* 2 (1922), 337-350, René Galland gives a brief analysis of the Dutch poet's life and works. He suggests (p. 339) that van der Noot was forced to earn his living by writing, having been deprived of his wealth during the religious wars. The most current presentation of the various versions of van der Noot's *Theatre* is W. A. P. Smit's *Het Bosken in Het Theatre* (Amsterdam: W. Vermeer, 1953).

(6) Galland, *ibid.,* p. 342, points out that the German edition was translated by Balthasar Froe who eliminated the violent passages addressed to Rome. This edition did not initiate any new movement of visionary poetry in Germany.

treatise from *Het Theatre* translated into French by van der Noot himself. When producing the English version, *A Theatre for Worldlings*, van der Noot engaged the services of two Englishmen. A certain Theodore Roest was the translator of the prose, who declared, to the confusion of Spenser scholars, that he had translated everything in the *Theatre* from the Dutch text. (7) Referring to the visions of Petrarch, he claims: «I have out of the Brabants speache turned them into the Englishe tongue.» (8) Possibly the confusion arises because Roest too literally translates the prose in the French text, but whatever the source of the confusion, investigation has demonstrated that Roest most certainly was not the translator of the poetry nor was the English verse based on the Dutch, although there is evidence that the translator may have consulted both the Dutch and the Italian, either directly or through an interpreter. (9)

Scholars generally agree that Edmund Spenser, still a school boy and accustomed to this sort of literary activity by his training, put Marot's «Visions de Pétrarque» as they appeared in the *Théâtre* and the eleven sonnets from Du Bellay's *Songe* into English verse. (10) Although we have no examples of

---

(7) No one has discovered the identity of Theodore Roest. See Louis S. Friedland, «Spenser's Minor Poems,» Diss. New York University, 1912, pp. iii-x.

(8) Jan van der Noot, *A Theatre for Voluptuous Worldlings* (New York: Scholars' Facsimiles, n. d.), p. cl.

(9) W. J. B. Pienaar, «Edmund Spenser and Jonker van der Noot,» *ES*, 8 (1926), 33-44, 67-76. See also Harold Stein, *Studies in Spenser's Complaints* (New York: Oxford Univ. Press, 1934), pp. 118-125.

(10) E. Koeppel, «Über die Echtheit der Edmund Spenser zugeschriebenen Visions of Petrarch und Visions of Bellay,» *Englische Studien*, 27 (1903), 100-111, tries to prove that Spenser did not translate the verse in the *Theatre*. However, J. B. Fletcher, «Spenser's Earliest Translations,» *JEGP*, 13 (1914), 305-308, claims that Koeppel tends to disprove his own case by finding elements in the poetry that are typical of Spenser. See also J. B. Fletcher, «Spenser and the *Theatre of Worldlings*,» *MLN*, 13 (1898), 409-415. and Louis S. Friedland, «Spenser's Earliest Translations,» *JEGP*, 12 (1913), 449-470. Alfred W. Satterthwaite, *Spenser, Ronsard, and Du*

6

Spenser's verse prior to 1569 when *A Theatre for Worldlings* appeared, already apparent poetic talent and a preference for moralistic writings may have prompted the Dutch poet to select Spenser as his translator. (11) We do not know the exact conditions under which Spenser translated the poems from the French emblem book, but it is certain that Spenser's early experience with this type of literary endeavor guided him throughout his career in both poetic theory and practice.

While dedicating the *Theatre,* the first English emblem book, to Elizabeth, van der Noot describes his work as a little treatise on «the vileness and baseness of worldely things, whiche commonly withdraw us from heavenly and spirituall matters,» and presents the book to the end «that understanding the vanitie and baseness of the same, and therewithall consideryng the miserable calamities that ensue therupon, we might be moved the rather to forsake them, and gyve oure selves to the knowledge of Heavenly and eternall things, whence all true happiness and felicitie doth procede.» (12) Although van der Noot was a poet of real merit, it was his Protestant zeal which inspired the *Theatre.* The images of Laura and those of Rome are therein transformed into the tools of anti-Catholic propaganda which warns especially that pride is bound to fall. (13) In this book, the visions, seen as examples of overweening pride, are treated in a more explicitly

---

Bellay: *A Renaissance Comparison* (Princeton: Princeton Univ. Press, 1960), pp. 255-263 (rpt. from *PQ*, 38 [1959], 509-515), has perhaps laid to rest this argument by attempting to prove Spenser's authorship of the visions through a study of «end-stops.» Satterthwaite (p. 255) claims that Spenser translated the epigrams and the eleven sonnets from *Songe* but not the four apocalyptic sonnets. He suggests that van der Noot may have done this himself.

(11) Pienaar, «Edmund Spenser and Jonker van der Noot,» pp. 67-76, suggests similarities in temperament and poetic practice between van der Noot and Spenser: an interest in moral allegory, Protestant leanings, and parallels between the Dutch poet's *Olympiados* and both the House of Pride and the Cave of Mammon in *The Faerie Queene*.

(12) Van der Noot, *Theatre*, pp. iii-iv.

(13) *Ibid.*, pp. xviii ff.

religious manner than they ever had been or would be in the works of Edmund Spenser. Nonetheless, van der Noot's evangelism seems to be directed to correcting human behavior. All this must have appealed to Spenser, who constantly returns to consider the problem implicit in the poetry of the *Theatre*. Eventually, he makes his own contribution to the visionary family, using the sonnet for something other than the subject of love.

In 1591, about twenty years after the publication of *A Theatre for Worldlings,* a volume entitled *Complaints Containing Sundrie Small Poemes of the Worlds Vanitie* came from the press of William Ponsonby. In the address to the reader, the printer describes the poems as sharing «like matter of argument» and as being «very grave and profitable.» (14) Like van der Noot's *Theatre,* Spenser's *Complaints* respond to a taste for melancholy, moralizing literature characteristic of early Renaissance England, which still preferred such complaints and tragedies as Chaucer's *Monk's Tale,* Lydgate's *Fall of Princes,* or Sackville's *Mirrour for Magistrates.* (15) Spenser's works reflect the taste of the times. William Nelson says that the *Complaints* contain the germ of Spenser's greater works and express a feeling of the world's vanity which «arises from a sense of the inevitable decay of sublunary things.» (16)

It is fitting that Spenser should have placed his various translations and imitations of Petrarch, Marot, and Du Bellay in such a volume. Returning to the work of his youth, Spenser puts them among his *Complaints* as *The Visions of Bellay* and *The Visions of Petrarch,* titles probably derived from Marot. We also find in this collection a translation of *Les Antiquitez de Rome* under the title *Ruines of Rome: by Bellay.* However, Spenser's interest in this sort of poetry does not stop with

---

(14) *The Works of Edmund Spenser,* p. 33.

(15) Anne Prescott, «The Reputation of Clément Marot in Renaissance England,» *SRen,* 18 (1971), 173-202, explains that Marot's reception in England illustrates the didactic emphasis of English critics, scholars, poets, and readers.

(16) *The Poetry of Edmund Spenser: A Study* (New York: Columbia Univ. Press, 1963), p. 64.

translations. In the *Complaints,* Spenser usually creates an original work to go with each translation. Besides the *Ruines of Rome,* he wrote the *Ruines of Time,* which includes two short sets of visions in the manner of the *Songe.* Besides *The Visions of Bellay* and *The Visions of Petrarch,* Spenser wrote *Visions of the worlds vanitie,* seemingly inspired by Du Bellay's use of Ecclesiastes.

The composition of the *Complaints* suggests that English poets, like their counterparts on the continent, considered imitation and translation an important part of the poetic process and one means of rivaling the ancients. Spenser was very much influenced by the Pléiade in France and by Du Bellay in particular. Nowhere is Du Bellay's inspiration more apparent than in *The Teares of the Muses,* a complaint about the low state to which poetry has fallen in England and also a kind of manifesto for the new poetry in England. The vision poems and the complaints are representative of a period in Spenser's career when he was attempting to find his way in a language that was still changing. Part of this process of change involved the assimilation of foreign words as well as the imitation of literary techniques and forms in the manner advocated by the Pléiade.

Some of the problems facing the English poets at the threshold of the Renaissance are very evident in the poetry of the *Theatre.* For example, the sonnet form had not yet become completely acclimatized in England and the poetic language still lacked a stable mode of versification. At this early stage of his career, Edmund Spenser had not yet found his own solutions, and his efforts in the *Theatre* are inconsistent. The meter of the epigrams is a somewhat uneven iambic pentameter; they are rhymed after the manner of the Surrey sonnet, later used by Shakespeare, although only two of them contain fourteen full lines and could be properly called Elizabethan sonnets. These translations have inaccurately been described as blank verse, (17) having been confused with the sonnets

_____

(17) Some critics, such as Fletcher, «Spenser and the *Theatre*

of Du Bellay, which, according to J. B. Fletcher, «prove Spenser at the tender age of seventeen the most finished maker of blank verse before Marlowe.» (18)

These early translations are quite literal, and the epigrams show that Spenser was using Marot's text. (19) For example, in the vision of the phoenix, Spenser follows Marot's word order without twisting English syntax:

> Au boys je vey un seul phenix portant
> Aesles de pourpre, et le chef tout doré:
> Estrange estoit, dont pensay en l'instant
> Veoir quelque corps celeste, jusque à tant
> Qu'il vint à l'arbre en pieces demouré,
> Et au ruisseau que terre a devoré.
> Que diray plus? Toute chose enfin passe:
>
> (lines 52-55)

> I saw a Phoenix in the wood alone,
> With purple wings and crest of golden hew,
> Straunge birde he was, whereby I thought anone,
> That of some heauenly wight I had the vew:
> Vntill he came vnto broken tree
> And to the spring that late deuoured was.
> What say I more? Eche thing at length we see
> Doth passe away:
>
> (*Epigrams,* lines 53-60)

Spenser seems to follow Petrarch in the brevity of his description of the tree as *«broken.»* However, he follows Marot

---

for Worldlings,» p. 415; Nelson, *ibid.,* p. 66; and Angelo Righetti, «Le due versioni spenseriane della canzone CCCXXIII del Petrarca,» *ACF,* 5 (1966), 117, have described the verse in the *Epigrams* incorrectly.

(18) Fletcher, «Spenser and the *Theatre of Worldlings,*» p. 415.

(19) Detailed comparisons of the epigrams of Marot, Spenser, and Petrarch's *canzone* can be found in B. Nicholson, «Spenser's Visions of Petrarch,» *NQ,* 7 (1887), 262-263; Friedland, «Spenser's

---

almost phrase for phrase and adds the rhetorical question that does not occur in the original. Spenser, like Marot, uses the generic term tree or *arbre* rather than the specific *alloro*.

At times, Spenser's verses almost equal the music and grace of the original usually lost in Marot. In the description of the fountain, Petrarch's allusion to the musical harmony is brief but marked by its internal rhymes. From Marot's rather flat and prosaic rendering Spenser creates equally lengthy but musical lines:

> Ma ninfe e muse, a quel tenor cantando:

> Mais mainte Muse et Nymphe seulement,
> Qui de leurs voix accordoient doulcement
> Au son de l'eau.

> But many Muses, and the Nymphes withall,
> That sweetely in accorde did tune their voice
> Vnto the gentle sounding of the waters fall.
> *(Epigrams,* lines 45-47)

The last line reveals the yet unsteady hand of the poet; it is irregular, containing twelve rather than the regular ten syllables.

Certain other elements in this early poetry have come to be considered typically Spenserian. At the beginning of his career, Spenser shows himself to be a student of language and a poet preparing his own poetic idiom, a suitable tool by which to express his individual fantasies. Veré L. Rubel finds examples of Spenser's early interest in poetic archaisms in the epigrams and sonnets: grisly, leames, welkin, whilome, yshrouded. Further, he finds such shortened past participles as astonned and erect, such —y adjectives as creekie, scaly, sunny,

---

Earliest Translations,» pp. 449-470; Pienaar, «Edmund Spenser and Jonker van der Noot,» pp. 33-44; and Stein, *Studies in Spenser's Complaints,* pp. 126-129.

and such compounds of adverb as outbrast, outgushing, and overcast. (20)

These poems must have held a particular appeal for Spenser because he revises them and gives them a prominent place in his *Complaints*; they stand as the finale to this entire collection. The visions are included in the section which was dedicated to Lady Carey (21) entitled *Muiopotmos*. *Muiopotmos* is the story of the tragic death of the exquisite butterfly Clarion, who like his mother Astery, is beset by the jealousy and envy of his enemies. Although *Muiopotmos* has been read as a personal or political allegory, its most obvious theme concerns the fall of proud beauty, and its art shows a relation to and advance beyond the brief metaphorical descriptions of the visions.

The art of *The Visions of Petrarch* and *The Visions of Bellay* is, of course, derivative. However, as we have seen, these works exhibit some of the most obvious aspects of Spenser's maturer style and reflect the state of the English language and literature of the time. Angelo Righetti sees a considerable difference between the epigrams and the *Visions of Petrarch*. He calls the *Epigrams* of 1569 translation «vera e propria,» which coincides «con un periodo di approfondimento del bagaglio culturale di un poeta e con un periodo di iniziazione artistica»; he sees the version of 1591 as an example of stylistic experimentation and interpretation where the «testo originale viene più interpretato che tradotto ... explicata in modo tale da farlo diventare un qualcosa di completamente nuovo.» (22) Righetti explains the change by an «affinamento poetico personale .... una rilettura attenta del Petrarca e il sommarsi di varie e profonde esperienze culturali che vanno dallo studio

---

(20) See Veré L. Rubel, *Poetic Diction in the English Renaissance from Skelton through Spenser* (New York: MLA, 1941), pp. 222-223.

(21) The *Complaints* is composed of several groups of poems dedicated individually to the Ladies Strange, Compton, and Carey and the Countesse of Pembroke.

(22) Righetti, «Le due versioni spenseriane,» p. 115.

degli umanisti a quello dei rinascimentali e dei manieristi.» (23) However, it seems that Righetti greatly overstates his case. He assumes both that the revisions were done during the time that Spenser wrote the first three books of the *Faerie Queen* and that the primary source for Spenser's translations was Petrarch's *canzone*. But Spenser scholars have never determined the exact date of the revisions and agree that the English epigrams are based mainly on Marot.

It is true that Spenser made some important changes while converting the sonnets of the *Theatre* to *The Visions of Bellay*. He reworks the sonnets into rhymed Elizabethan sonnets and also translates, for the first time, sonnets 6, 8, 13, and 14 of *Songe* which had been omitted by van der Noot. (24) The few attempts at rhetoric in the earlier poems are not retained in the *Visions*. The changes in language cause Veré L. Rubel to believe that the revisions show Spenser experimenting toward the language of *The Faerie Queene*. (25)

For the most part, the style of *The Visions of Petrarch* shows no significant evolution. Spenser, an unusually careful translator, makes few textual alterations other than changing the spelling and recasting four of the epigrams as sonnets, which sometimes requires that the poet modify the final lines of the epigrams in order to maintain the correct rhyme and syntax. Since Spenser had originally rhymed the epigrams, very few major alterations were required. By this time, he is better able to regulate the number of accents and syllables in his verse, and he finds a way to revise that particularly harmonious passage in the vision of the fountain and to emphasize the alliteration involving the sibilants so notable in Petrarch's poem. Evincing little regard for the logical structure of the Surreyan sonnet, the first six sonnets in *The Visions of Petrarch* lack an effective formal organization. The somewhat numerous

---

(23) *Ibid.*, p. 118.
(24) Stein, *Studies in Spenser's Complaints*, pp. 151-167.
(25) Rubel, *Poetic Diction in the English Renaissance*, pp. 222-223.

spelling changes in the revision suggest once again Spenser's interest in language. (26)

As we have seen, the metaphorical value of the central images is somewhat transformed when the poem is first removed from the context of the *Canzoniere* by Marot. Spenser is greatly influenced by Marot, and follows him in omitting certain crucial modifiers. Although Spenser's revisions indicate that he may have consulted the Italian text, he does not attempt to reestablish the original meaning of the metaphors. In the first vision, he follows Marot in deleting the phrase «con fronte umana»:

> Una fera m'apparve da man destra
> *Con fronte umana* da far arder Giove,

> Si m'apparut une bische a main destre,
> *Belle* pour plaire au souverain des dieux.

> At my right hand a Hynde appear'd to mee,
> So *faire* as mote the greatest God delite, (27)
>   (*The Visions of Petrarch,* lines 4-5, italics are mine)

When unable to translate word for word, Marot paraphrases or expands the original according to the requirements of syntax, rhyme, and sense. Likewise, Spenser alters the poetry to fulfill the requirements of the sonnet form, and ultimately reveals his interpretation of the visionary experience. Although the *Epigrams* and *The Visions of Petrarch* are almost identical, Spenser's additions emphasize and expand the sententious phrases of the original. The English poet's reactions are not a response to the death of his beloved; rather, they reflect this preoccupation with the mutable common throughout Spenser's poetry. For instance Spenser replaces the «Ahi nulla altro che

---

(26) Friedland, «Spenser's Earliest Translations,» p. 465.
(27) These lines quoted from *The Visions of Petrarch* differ from the *Epigrams* in spelling only.

pianto al mondo dura!» with a quartet of lines that shows the influence of Du Bellay's «torment»:

> Alas, on earth so nothing doth endure,
> But bitter griefe and sorrowfull annoy:
> Which make this life wretched and miserable,
> Tossed with stormes of fortune variable.
> *(The Visions of Petrarch, lines 81-84)*

The elaboration expresses not merely a lover's dismay, but includes the whole of the bitter earthly experience.

Unlike Marot, Spenser does not confine himself to translation but injects new life into the form and content of the visionary poem with the *Vision of the worlds vanitie*. Spenser turns to consider that element of disorder in nature which can disturb the happiness of any creature no matter how well endowed. His theme is the weakness of the phenomenal world and his illustration of the world's vanities is quite different from Du Bellay's. In its structure and style, *Visions of the worlds vanitie* reveals something about Spenser's eclectic poetic methods, his catholic tastes, his conscious interest in developing an unusual diction, and his proclivity for graphic, pictorial writing. We perceive the various influences of the French and Italian visions as well as of the traditions of moralistic verse such as those which used animals to demonstrate human behavior. Of course, Spenser exercises his inventive faculties and produces a series of visions that is singularly Spenserian.

All these poets have given us sophisticated, learned meditations, but Spenser alone conveys this in an introductory exposition without couching his experience in the guise of a dream or vision. The first quatrain reveals both the nature of his experience and the subject of the poem:

> One day, whiles that my daylie cares did sleepe,
> My spirit, shaking off her earthly prison,

Began to enter into meditation deepe
Of things exceeding reach of common reason;
            (*Vision of the worlds vanitie* 1, lines 1-4)

In the following quatrains, which develop these ideas,
the poet suggests that the weakness inherent in the most
worthy and the meanest of earthly creatures is an aspect of
earthly existence beyond the reach of reason alone. Hence, the
«strange showes» presenting themselves to the seer's eyes are
explained as proceeding from a mystical experience in which
the ironies of life are translated into concrete images:

Vnto my eyes strange showes presented were,
Picturing that, which I in minde embraced,
That yet those sights empassion me full nere.
    (*Visions of the worlds vanitie* 1, lines 10-12)

Spenser retains the notion of «Standomi un giorno» that
memory powerfully affects the emotions. However, he expresses more than the personal concern of the lover. Spenser
accentuates the positive and admonishes the «faire Ladie» to
heed the lessons of the visions in the hope that they may be
of some benefit in future circumstances:

Such as they were (faire Ladie) take in worth,
That when time serues, may bring things better forth.
    (*Visions of the worlds vanitie* 1, lines 13-14)

As he modifies the structure, so he modifies the selection
of images and the nobility of the subject. Where Petrarch's
images were noble, dignified creations and Du Bellay's were
inspired by the paradox of the grandeur and ruin of Rome,
Spenser's images are exclusively animals, a subject Alfred
Satterthwaite terms «both monstrous and petty.» In comparison to Du Bellay, Satterthwaite believes that Spenser has
dehumanized his subject and has presented it in a pedestrian

manner. (28) In reality, some of Spenser's creatures, the crocodile, the dragon, the figure of *Leuiathan,* are reminiscent of those manneristic tendencies in *Songe,* albeit they are presented rather plainly in face of the richer texture of Du Bellay's rhetoric. Other images derive primarily from natural history and fables, while still others derive from the visions of Petrarch and Du Bellay. There are the cedar whose legendary properties make it the sister of the laurel, the Eagle, who dares lay his eggs in Jove's lap, the image of Rome saved by a goose, and the ubiquitous image of the ship.

As a student at the Merchant Taylor's School, Spenser undoubtedly gained the background which made him, as Friedland puts it, «the foremost *English* fabulist of his time.» (29) Certain sonnets in *Visions of the worlds vanitie* come from the world of fable. Both sonnet 2, concerning a bull and a gadfly, and sonnet 10, concerning a lion and a wasp, are akin to the fable of a gadfly who overcomes a large, savage beast. Sonnet 4, the vision of the eagle and the scarabee, is based upon a well known fable, while sonnet 8 is a variation of the fable about the elephant and the mouse. (30)

In these animal visions, the moralistic summary common to fable appears in the short refrain which leaves much to the imagination. The moral is never directly stated, however, because the «pictures» are revelatory. In both fable and vision, a relationship between two animals is depicted, but the visions are entirely composed of poetic description rather than dialogue. Like his predecessors, Spenser uses abstract description of moral or internal traits to advantage. The poet is

---

(28) «Moral Vision in Spenser, Du Bellay, and Ronsard,» *CL,* 9 (1957), 140.

(29) Louis S. Friedland, «Spenser as a Fabulist,» *The Shakespeare Association Bulletin,* 12 (1937), 207. Elsewhere (pp. 89-92), Friedland discusses the popularity of Aesop as a textbook in sixteenth-century schools.

(30) *Ibid.,* p. 198.

concerned with the practical didactic value of his poetry as are the writers of fables or bestiaries, where human attributes are ascribed to animals in order to correct behavior, to moralize, and to expound church doctrine. Spenser, however, is primarily interested in the matter of human behavior.

A comparison of the poetic technique in the two sonnets resembling the fable of the weak creature who defeats a truculent and powerful opponent shows Spenser's ability to vary the structure of his visions. In the second sonnet, there is a bull who is privileged not only because of his singular appearance but also because of his paradisiacal habitat. Although this bull is «as white as driuen snowe, / With gilden hornes,» a symbol of purity, innocence, and beauty, his fortune is desirable only

> Till that a Brize, a scorned little creature,
> Through his faire hide his angrie sting did threaten,
> And vext so sore, that all his goodly feature,
> And all his plenteous pasture nought him pleased:
> (*Visions of the worlds vanitie* 2, lines 24-27)

In all the vision poems, Spenser observes the curious fact that small causes bring about great misfortunes. Spenser's creatures are not ordinarily destroyed, nor do they undergo metamorphoses. Rather, they are left in severe distress. The bull's nemesis is a «scorned little creature,» which is capable of turning abundant pleasure to sorrowful dissatisfaction: «So by the small the great is oft diseased» (2, line 28).

Animal imagery is common throughout this collection of *Complaints*. The image of the bull, the first of Spenser's visions, appears to be a cameo of the tale of the butterfly Clarion in *Muiopotmos*. It is possible that Spenser intended *Visions of the worlds vanitie* to complement the other original poem in this group, *Muiopotmos,* as Du Bellay's *Songe* had complemented *Les Antiquitez de Rome*. In *Muiopotmos*, Clarion, the protagonist, meets a cruel fate through envy, circumstance, and the natural enmity of Aragnoll, the spider.

(31) Likewise, the visions portray both the beautiful and the unsightly.

Spenser, like Du Bellay, depicts his images in a variety of attitudes. The lion's fierce majesty contrasts with the mellow beauty of the bull, but his «cruell clawes» are no match for the wasp, which can make life so odious that its larger opponent desires death: «So weakest may anoy the most of might» (10, line 140). Spenser cites an example of symbiosis from Pliny; his third sonnet describes the natural inter-dependency of the crocodile and the crocodile bird, which Spenser calls *Tedula*. (32) By contrasting the ferocity and enormity of the crocodile with the smallness and fragility of the bird, the «least of thousands which on earth abide,» Spenser illustrates the nature of the earthly condition. It is the very nature of things that no earthly creature is without its weakness or its need. And help or destruction may come from the least expected source.

Spenser's visions rely on exaggeration and repetition for their effect. The images are not properly symbols or metaphors of the types found in «Standomi un giorno» or *Songe*. Spenser limits the sensuousness and decoration of his images. In sonnet 5, for instance, he introduces Leviathan, «huge,» «Natures wonder,» an animal of the «dreadfull deep,» which seems to be the source of the waves in the sea. He appeals more

---

(31) Friedland, *ibid.*, p. 197, says that *Muiopotmos* is based on the fable of «The Flea and the Man» as well as on the metamorphosis of Arachne. Spenser's modification of the myth of Arachne serves to delineate the lineage of his hero's enemy as well as to suggest the tragic outcome of his tale. Spenser introduces the butterfly as the crowning touch of Minerva's tapestry which proves her superior to her mortal rival Arachne. Seeing this evidence, Arachne swells up from rage and envy and is transformed into a spider. Thus, the emotion of Arachne's progeny, Aragnoll, towards Clarion, the butterfly hero, is quite natural.

(32) Spenser, always more interested in the action or behavior of a creature than in scientific, historical, or literary accuracy, seems to have created this name, perhaps having forgotten the proper form of the term, trochilus. This is another example of his freehanded use of his sources.

directly than Du Bellay to our sense of awe before nature's mysterious forces.

A consideration of the images which occur in every series of visions reveals the basic differences in techniques and in outlooks of the various poets. Spenser's visions are a product of his early years, whereas Petrarch, Marot, and Du Bellay's poems come from the years of their maturity. Nonetheless, the imagery which the youthful Spenser appropriates from the popular tradition of beast fables remains an integral part of the fantasy which later produces *The Faerie Queene*. (33) Contrastingly, the imagery of Petrarch and Du Bellay is noble, aristocratic, deriving from the humanistic tradition. These elements are not wholly absent from *Visions of the worlds vanitie,* but neither are they dominant. Spenser's vision of a ship betrays this difference in class. His is not the stately ship of Petrarch bedecked in gold, ivory, and ebony, loaded with rich merchandise, nor is it Du Bellay's even more richly outfitted vessel. Spenser's ship is

> A goodly ship with banners brauely dight,
> ... ...
> Through the maine sea making her merry flight:
> ... ...
> she did seeme to daunce, as in delight,
> And at her owne felicitie did smile
> > (*Visions of the worlds vanitie* 9, lines 114,
> > 116, 119-120)

The concrete detail is lacking, and the ship is a rather straight-forward personification of a merry and lighthearted soul.

The relationships depicted in these visions do not always beget destruction because the thematic focus of *Visions of the worlds vanitie* is other than mutability; Spenser concentrates on those more common and natural pitfalls in life which we

---

(33) Madeleine Pelner Cosman, «Spenser's Ark of Animals: Animal Imagery in *The Faerie Queene*,» *SEL,* 3 (1963), 85-107.

cannot avoid but for which we can prepare ourselves. Of all those qualities which may be desirable (i.e., power, beauty, mystery, size, danger, security, happiness), (34) not one is without its vulnerability. Spenser tries to define the paradoxical quality of earthly greatness, subject to the laws of nature and to change which governs the world. A very weak, small creature is used as the agent of change in every vision, emphasizing the fragility of good fortune.

With its archaisms of diction, the decorative alliteration, and the visionary form itself, Spenser's poem has a markedly quaint flavor. A sense of remoteness from the everyday world, from naturalism, is produced by Spenser's mannerisms, and makes the reader more conscious of a didactic intent. Nearly every sonnet contains antiquated vocabulary such as cleepe, brust, sith, dreadles, hap, dight, surquedrie. This special coloration is almost absent from his French forerunners and even from Petrarch.

As Petrarch and Du Bellay had selected imagery befitting their individual subjects, so Spenser selects images which will direct the reader's mind to the universal truth that the «weakest may anoy the most of might» (10, line 140). Typically, the English poet is most greatly concerned with the relationship between his images and the theme for which they furnish appropriate pictorial representations. (35) Rejecting Viglione's suggestions that Spenser's visions are a «glorificazione delle classi meno abbienti» (36) or symbols of «la superbia di Roma papale,» in the manner of van der Noot, (37) Alfred W. Satterthwaite suggests that the emphasis on the fall of pride is a moral rather than a social concern and that the work

---

(34) W. L. Renwick, *Edmund Spenser*: *An Essay on Renaissance Poetry* (London: Arnold, 1925), p. 265, calls these visions «parables of power.»

(35) Rosemond Tuve, *Elizabethan and Metaphysical Imagery*, p. 40, and especially pp. 145-155.

(36) F. Viglione, *La poesia lirica di Edmondo Spenser* (Genoa: Orfini, 1937), p. 130.

(37) *Ibid.*, pp. 129-130.

is didactic though never specifically religious. (38) Hence, when the poet presents his conclusions in the twelfth sonnet, he exhorts the reader to «read these ruines tragicall» and «Learne by their losse to loue the low degree» (12, lines 164-165). Reflecting a theme common throughout Spenser's works, the moralistic tone of *Visions of the worlds vanitie* culminates in the warning that the principle of life is change-ability, and that whoever «of himselfe is most secure, / Shall finde his state most fickle and vnsure» (12, lines 167-168).

This is not Spenser's last word on the subject of man's «tickle trustles state.» *The Visions of Petrarch* which originally inspired all this poetry are placed at the end of the *Complaints* and contain a closing sonnet which serves as an epilogue, at least to the whole group of poems dedicated to Lady Carey. This last sonnet does not share the Surreyan structure of *The Visions of Petrarch* and is better viewed as a general summation in which the poet concludes that he could gladly leave this earthly life for his spiritual resting place, a proposi-tion that reappears at the end of the «Cantos of Mutabilitie» in *The Faerie Queene* (7.8.2). Not entirely in contrast with that Petrarchan sonnet which inspires its first lines («Quand' io mi volgo in dietro a mirar gli anni» [298]), Spenser's sonnet is both intimate and hortatory, addressed to the lady with the hope that the examples will prompt her own reflections and correct her attitudes toward the nature of the world as they had the poet's.

In Spenser's visions, we find an urgent note and the sug-gestion that earthly life can be lived fully and profitably in the time allotted to us, as long as we are prepared for the fickleness of fortune. Broadly speaking, the emphasis of Spenser's poetry is far removed from the visions of his predecessors. Spenser's stance is quite positive; his visions are not so much poems of love or philosophy as of instruction. Even his translations of Petrarch and Du Bellay are endowed with a magisterial tone

---

(38) «Moral Vision in Spenser, Du Bellay, and Ronsard,» pp. 138-141.

7

when they appear in the *Complaints*. Spenser's is the more practical, less transcendental vision of man who should be concerned with living wisely by his own means in spite of his individual or natural weaknesses. With a tone that is almost encouraging, he leaves us with the hope of some benefit to be derived from an understanding of the world.

Spenser is the last of the notable European poets to find this visionary method compatible with his mode of thought and mode of writing. He gives us in the *Complaints* the most important Renaissance collection of poems on the transcience of earthly things. He translates, he imitates, and he seemingly exhausts the possibilities of the Petrarchan vision. Although Spenser later creates several visionary sequences in the more complex and elaborate narrative of *The Faerie Queene,* he never again turns to the short vision poem. In the decades after the publication of the *Complaints,* these visions in the Petrarchan manner disappear, never to return.

CHAPTER VI

CONCLUSION: OUTSIDE THE CONVENTIONS
OF LOVE

With his «Standomi un giorno,» Petrarch initiated the growth of a major family of poems which flourished for several decades during the sixteenth century, yet did not participate in the ascendance of Petrarch as a poet of love. The general nature of the poem's history abroad does not differ radically from that of the other *Rime* but precedes it. Indeed, the influence of the visions bridges the two later waves of Petrarchism in Europe, the impact of the *Trionfi* and the impact of the *Canzoniere*. (1) After its translation into French by Marot, the *canzone* had a considerable development for a poem that is still regarded by some as one of Petrarch's lesser works. Maggini, undoubtedly echoing De Sanctis, says that it is «una poesia del Petrarca che non è delle più alte.» (2) But it is precisely the modern sensibility which produces this judgment; the poets and readers of the early Renaissance evidently read and appreciated its form and its matter. The imitators of «Standomi un giorno» used this poem for stylistic experimentation or for displaying poetic virtuosity. Their

---

(1) For a discussion of the three waves of Petrarch's influence, see E. H. Wilkins, «A General Survey of Renaissance Petrarchism» in his *Studies in the Life and Works of Petrarch*, pp. 280-299.
(2) Maggini, p. 47.

modifications in style and subject lent interest and variety to this body of poems, but not the type of interest that would sustain this family of poems in the developing Renaissance.

«Standomi un giorno» falls outside the mainstream of the influence of the *Canzoniere,* and, therefore, represents a rather special form of Petrarch's influence. Although it is one of the love lyrics, *canzone* 323 is almost a triumph in miniature, a pageant which portrays Laura's death, the poet's grief at her passing, and his sensitivity to the transitoriness of created things. It could be transformed either into a vision of the fall of Rome or into a vision of the frailties of creatures. Because of their graphic metaphors and their quasi-moralistic tone, such visions also profited by the initial vogue of the emblem books. Had they not been popularized by van der Noot, the visions might have died out even sooner than they did. Van der Noot incorporated the visions of Petrarch and Du Bellay into his *Theatre,* an emblem book compiled and edited in Dutch, French, English and German. Having translated the poems for the English version, Edmund Spenser was prompted to write several sets of visions in his *Complaints.* However, when Balthasar Froe translated the poems into German, his translations inspired no original adaptations.

These visionary poems were easily brought into the emblem tradition because they exemplified the original definition of an emblem. Andrea Alciati started this literary fashion with his *Emblemata,* a collection of epigrams dating from 1521. (3) According to Hessel Miedema, Alciati defined an emblem as «an epigram in which something specific is described in such a way as to give additional meaning ('significet') to a pleasant but fortuitous fact or phenomenon; or: in such a way that

---

(3) Hessel Miedema, «The Term *Emblema* in Alciati,» *JWCI*, 31 (1968), 237, explains that «in the third decade of the sixteenth century, in the high aristocratic circles in Milan to which Alciati belonged, the compiling of collections of *emblemata,* or poetry and epigrams, was in fashion. Ambrogio Visconti is named as the originator of the idea; Alciati and Albuzi produced them.» Alciati's is the first known book of emblems to be published.

what is described comes to indicate something else and thereby itself acquires a pleasing moral.» (4) Undoubtedly, this sort of literature had its origins in the Renaissance love of allegory and the assumption that the literary artist could appeal to his reader by word and by picture. (5) It was, as Miedema notes, the publisher who eventually added illustrations to Alciati's emblems as a guide for the less educated reader. (6) Since the habit of publishing manuscripts with illustrations dates from medieval times, such editing seems inevitable. The visions were easily illustrated by means of woodcuts and adapted to the purposes of the *Theatre*. (7)

That van der Noot found a relevant content in these visions, there can be no doubt. In the prose treatise of the *Theatre*, he analyzes the poem as an expression of earthly vanity and as a rejection of romantic love. He relates that Petrarch had loved Laura honestly for twenty-one years until her death, after which he mourned the space of ten years, and composed many sorrowful poems including the visionary «Standomi un giorno.» (8) Dividing the *canzone* into two sections, van der Noot sees three poems which refer directly to Laura's death, and three which are to be read as general examples of the

---

(4) *Ibid.*, p. 241.

(5) A medieval writer, Richart de Fornival, *Li Bestiares d'Amours di Maistre Richart di Fornival e li Response du Bestiaire*, ed. Cesare Segre (Milan: Ricciardi, 1957), pp. 3-5, says that there are two ways of learning, by word and by picture, and that in his bestiary he uses both methods of impressing the reader. In «What Is an Emblem?» *JAAC*, 29 (1970), 261, Elizabeth K. Hill notes that «emblems share with conceits, symbols and other figures a type of thinking inherited from the Middle Ages.»

(6) Miedema, p. 243. He also explains (pp. 245-247) that during the decade following the publication of the *Emblemata* by Heinrich Steyner, emblem books appeared sometimes with illustrations and sometimes without them. However, the practice of publishing emblems with illustrations became so established that after 1549 illustrations almost always accompanied the verses, though people were still aware that an emblem was really an epigram.

(7) See, for example, Louis Leeber, *L'Esprit de la gravure au XVe siècle* (Brussels, 1943), p. 15.

(8) Van der Noot, *Theatre*, p. xiii.

misery, sorrow, afflictions, and calamities which confront man in this imperfect world, a warning that men should not devote themselves to vain, earthly fantasies, including even beautiful virtuous women. Petrarch, says van der Noot, having spent a long ten years in mourning his lady, discovered that there was «no comfort, hope or salvation in worldely love to be loked for,» and «turned himself to Godwarde, lamenting and sorrowing the rest of hys life so ydlely and undecently spent.» (9) If this is a gauge of the sixteenth-century reader's interest in the poem, it suggests why the visions eventually were eclipsed, and why the last transformation of the *canzone* was a «Canción fúnebre,» written by Quevedo on the death of Luis Carillo in 1610. (10)

By this time, however, the simplistic emblematic method seemed less appropriate to the complexities dealt with either by religious poets or by love poets. Religious poets dealt with more specifically religious questions in an introspective but intellectual manner, sometimes turning to the Ignatian method of meditation which required the applications of the senses to aid in the comprehension of religious truths. Another aspect of Petrarchism came to be the primary influence on Renaissance poets, and it was no longer fashionable to view Petrarch either as a moralist or as a love poet in the manner of Dante. Both poets and emblematists began to shift from moralistic subjects with an outmoded manner of presentation to the more courtly or to the more philosophical concerns of love. As the model of courtly poetry, Petrarch provided a stylish mode of writing compliments and an adequate means of expressing the inward

(9) *Ibid.*, p. xi. Van der Noot's interpretation of the poem is suggestive, but his conclusions about this *canzone* may be motivated by his own purpose. Of course, at the end of the *Rime*, Petrarch writes several songs to the Virgin, which the Dutch poet could have interpreted as a palinode.

(10) *Obras completas de Don Francisco de Quevedo Villegas*, ed. Luis A. Marín (Madrid: Aguilar, 1932), II, 461-463.

experience of love. Since much of this poetry was a means of paying court to ladies, a poem on death would hardly have been suitable. Poets turned to Petrarch's method of courtship, his idea of a cycle of poems, his language, and to such devices as the eternizing conceit, finding in them a more timely and fruitful source of poetry. With this perceptible change in tastes, the visions finally grew wearisome and died.

SELECTED BIBLIOGRAPHY

Bergin, Thomas G. *Petrarch.* New York: Twayne, 1970.

Bentley-Cranch, Dana. «La réputation de Marot en Angleterre.» *SFr*, 50 (1973), 201-221.

Bernardo, Aldo S. *Petrarch, Laura, & The 'Triumphs'.* Albany: State Univ. of New York Press, 1974.

Calcaterra, Carlo. *Nella selva del Petrarca.* Bologna: Cappelli, 1942.

Chambers, Frank M. «Lucan and the *Antiquitez de Rome.*» *PMLA*, 60 (1945), 937-948.

Chiappelli, Fredi. «La canzone delle visioni e il sostrato tematico della 'fabula inexpleta'.» *GSLI*, 141 (1964), 321-335.

— «La canzone petrarchesca delle visioni.» *YIS*, 1 (1971), 235-247.

— *Studi sul linguaggio del Petrarca: La canzone delle visioni.* Florence: Olschki, 1971.

Cosman, Madeleine Pelner. «Spenser's Ark of Animals: Animal Imagery in *The Faerie Queene.*» *SEL*, 3 (1963), 85-107.

Durling, Robert M. *The Figure of the Poet in the Renaissance Epic.* Cambridge: Harvard Univ. Press, 1965.

Fletcher, J. B. «Spenser and the *Theatre for Worldlings.*» *MLN*, 13 (1898), 409-415.

— «Spenser's Earliest Translations.» *JEGP*, 13 (1914), 305-308.

Forster, Leonard. *The Icy Fire: Five Studies in European Petrarchism.* Cambridge: Cambridge Univ. Press, 1969.

Françon, Marcel. «Sur l'influence de Pétrarque en France aux XVe et XVIe siècles.» *Italica*, 19 (1942), 105-110.

— «Vasquin Philieul, traducteur de Pétrarque.» *FS*, 4 (1950), 216-226.

Friedland, Louis S. «Spenser as a Fabulist.» *The Shakespeare Association Bulletin*, 12 (1937), 85-108, 133-154, 197-207.

— «Spenser's Earliest Translations.» *JEGP*, 12 (1913), 449-470.

— «Spenser's Minor Poems.» Diss. New York Univ., 1912.

Galland, René. «Un poète errant de la Renaissance: Jean van der Noot et l'Angleterre.» *RLC*, 2 (1922), 337-350.

Jones, R. O. «Renaissance Butterfly, Mannerist Flea: Tradition and Change in Renaissance Poetry.» *MLN*, 80 (1965), 166-184.

Koeppel, E. «Über die Echtheit der Edmund Spenser zugeschriebenen Visions of Petrarch und Visions of Bellay.» *Englische Studien*, 27 (1903), 100-111.

Lapp, John C. «Mythological Imagery in Du Bellay.» *SP*, 61 (1964), 109-127.

Maggini, Francesco. «La canzone delle visioni.» *SPetr*, 1 (1948), 37-50.

Mayer, C. A. *Bibliographie des oeuvres de Clément Marot*. Geneva: Droz, 1954.

— and D. Bentley-Cranch. «Clément Marot, poète pétrarquiste.» *BHR*, 28 (1966), 32-51.

Miedema, Hessel. «The Term *Emblema* in Alciati.» *JWCI*, 31 (1968), 234-250.

Nelson, William. *The Poetry of Edmund Spenser: A Study*. New York: Columbia Univ. Press, 1963.

Nicholson, B. «Spenser's Visions of Petrarch.» *NQ*, 7 (1887), 262-263.

Noot, Jan van der. *A Theatre for Voluptuous Worldlings*. New York: Scholars' Facsimiles, n. d.

Pasqualigo, Francesco. *Le visioni del Petrarca nella canzone «Standomi un giorno» confrontati coi Trionfi dello stesso*. Rome: Bonghi, 1887.

Pienaar, W. J. B. «Edmund Spenser and Jonker van der Noot.» *ES*, 8 (1926), 33-44, 67-76.

Praz, Mario. *Ricerche anglo-italiane*. Rome: Istituto Grafico Tiberino, 1944.

— *Studies in Seventeenth-Century Imagery*. 2nd ed. Rome: Edizioni di Storia e Letteratura, 1964.

Prescott, Anne Lake. «The Reputation of Clément Marot in Renaissance England.» *SRen*, 18 (1971), 173-202.

Reichenberger, Kurt. «Das Italienerlebnis Du Bellays: Die Thematik des 'Songe' und seine Beziehung zur manieristischen Ideenwelt.» *ZfrPh*, 82 (1966), 261-266.

Renwick, W. L. *Edmund Spenser: An Essay on Renaissance Poetry*. London: Edward Arnold, 1925.

Righetti, Angelo. «Le due versioni spenseriane della canzone CCCXXIII del Petrarca.» *ACF*, 5 (1966), 115-122.

Rutson, E. M. «A Note on Jean Marot's Debt to Italian Sources.» *MLR*, 61 (1966), 25-28.

Saba, Guido. *La poesia di Joachim du Bellay*. Florence: D'Anna, 1962.

Satterthwaite, A. W. «Moral Vision in Spenser, Du Bellay, and Ronsard.» *CL*, 9 (1957), 136-149.

— «A Re-examination of Spenser's Translations of the 'Sonets' from *A Theatre for Worldlings*.» *PQ*, 38 (1959), 509-515.

— *Spenser, Ronsard, and Du Bellay: A Renaissance Comparison*. Princeton: Princeton Univ. Press, 1960.

Saulnier, V.-L. «Commentaires sur les *Antiquitez de Rome*.» *BHR*, 12 (1950), 114-143.

Scaglione, Aldo, ed. *Francis Petrarch, Six Centuries Later: A Symposium*. Univ. of North Carolina Studies in the Romance Languages and Literatures, Symposia No. 3. Chapel Hill: Univ. of North Carolina Press, 1975.

Simone, Franco. *Il Rinascimento francese: studi e ricerche*. Turin: Società Editrice Internazionale, 1961.

Smit, W. A. P. *Het Bosken en Het Theatre.* Amsterdam: W. Vermeer, 1953.

Smith, P. M. *Clément Marot: Poet of the French Renaissance.* London: Athlone Press, 1970.

Stein, Harold. *Studies in Spenser's Complaints.* New York: Oxford Univ. Press, 1934.

Vianey, Joseph. *Le Pétrarquisme en France au XVIe siècle.* Montpellier: Coulet, 1909.

Viglione, Francesco. *La poesia lirica di Edmondo Spenser.* Genoa: Emiliano degli Orfini, 1937.

Wardropper, Bruce W. *Historia de la poesia lyrica a lo divino en la cristiandad occidental.* Madrid: Revista de Occidente, 1958.

Wells, Margaret Brady. «Du Bellay's Sonnet Sequence, *Songe.*» *FS*, 26 (1972), 1-8.

Wilkins, Ernest Hatch. *Life of Petrarch.* Chicago: Univ. of Chicago Press, 1963.

— *The Making of the Canzoniere and other Petrarchan Studies.* Rome: Edizioni di Storia e Letteratura, 1951.

Se terminó de imprimir en
la Ciudad de Madrid en el
mes de Mayo de 1978.

studia humanitatis

FORTHCOMING PUBLICATIONS

El cancionero del Bachiller Jhoan Lopez, edición crítica de Rosalind Gabin.

LOPE DE VEGA, *El amor enamorado,* critical edition of John B. Wooldridge, Jr.

Studies in Honor of Gerald E. Wade, edited by Sylvia Bowman, Bruno M. Damiani, Janet W. Díaz, E. Michael Gerli, Everett Hesse, John E. Keller, Luis Leal and Russell Sebold.

HELMUT HATZFELD, *Essais sur la littérature flamboyante.*

MARIO ASTE, *La narrativa di Luigi Pirandello: Dalle novelle al romanzo «Uno, Nessuno, e Centomila».*

JOHN A. FREY, *The Aesthetics of the* ROUGON-MACQUART.

VINCENZO TRIPODI, *Studi su Foscolo e Stern.*

JOSEPH BARBARINO, *The Latin Intervocalic Stops: A Quantitative and Comparative Study.*

NANCY D'ANTUONO, *Boccaccio's novelle in Lope's theatre.*

ANTONIO PLANELLS, *Cortázar: Metafísica y erotismo.*

Novelistas femeninas de la postguerra española, ed. Janet W. Díaz.

MECHTHILD CRANSTON, *Orion Resurgent: René Char, Poet of Presence.*

La Discontenta and La Pythia, edition with introduction and notes by Nicholas A. De Mara.

NANCY DERSOFI, *Arcadia and the Stage: A Study of the Theater of Angelo Beolco (called Ruzante).*

PERO LÓPEZ DE AYALA, *Crónica del Rey Don Pedro I,* edición crítica de Heanon and Constance Wilkins.

ALBERT H. LE MAY, *The Experimental Verse Theater of Valle-Inclán.*

CHESTER W. OBUCHOWSKI, *Mars on Trial: War as Seen by French Writers of the Twentieth Century.*

JEREMY T. MEDINA, *Spanish Realism: Theory and Practice of a Concept in the Nineteenth Century.*

Robert H. Miller, ed. *Sir John Harington: A Supplie or Addicion to the «Catalogue of Bishops» to the Yeare 1608.*

María Elisa Ciavarelli, *La fuerza de la sangre en la literatura del Siglo de Oro.*

Mary Lee Bretz, *La evolución novelística de Pío Baroja.*

Dennis M. Kratz, *Mocking Epic.*